THE ULTIMATE SENIOR RETIREMENT GUIDE

Live a Purposeful, Active, and Connected Life With Practical and Inspirational Guidance

PAULINE WINSLOW

Contents

Introduction

As dawn casts its gentle light over a peaceful garden, where the only sounds are birdsong, and the rustle of leaves, the tranquility of the scene belies the undercurrent of apprehension many feel about entering retirement. This pivotal life stage, ripe with possibility, also brings its share of anxieties: financial security, maintaining health, and finding a new purpose. I know this paradox well through personal experience and the many voices I've listened to.

My name is Pauline Winslow, and I've traversed the landscape of retirement, encountering its challenges and embracing its opportunities. Drawing from a wealth of experiences—both my own and those of others—I've crafted this guide to help you navigate this significant transition. My goal is simple yet profound: to equip you with the knowledge and inspiration to live a fulfilling retirement.

Retirement is not just an end but a beginning—a chance to rediscover old passions, cultivate new interests, and strengthen connections in this digital age. Through this book, I invite you to journey with me as we explore practical financial strategies, explore exciting new hobbies, and learn how to stay connected and relevant in a rapidly evolving world.

I am deeply empathic about the rollercoaster of emotions that retirement can evoke and steadfastly dedicated to supporting you. Retirement offers a unique opportunity for growth, happiness, and purpose, and I am here to show you how it can be manageable and richly rewarding.

Structured to address every facet of retirement life, the chapters ahead will guide you through essential topics such as adjusting to changes in daily routines, managing health and wellness, and fostering meaningful relationships. Each section is designed to empower you, providing the tools and encouragement needed to make your retirement years vibrant and impactful.

My commitment to this subject is personal. I remember the mixed feelings of stepping away from my career: excitement tinged with uncertainty. It was a canvas waiting for new colors, but knowing which colors to choose was challenging. This book is borne out of those experiences and the lessons learned along the way.

It is crucial to approach retirement with an open mind and readiness to adapt. We'll cover diverse topics, from practical advice on downsizing to embracing technology, all tailored to help you thrive in this new phase of life.

Let's embark on this journey together with open hearts and minds. With the proper guidance and mindset, I assure you that retirement can be one of your life's most enjoyable and fulfilling times. Join me, and let's discover the rich rewards in your next chapter.

ONE

Embracing a New Identity

Stepping away from a career you've nurtured over decades can feel like leaving a long-term relationship. Suddenly, the routines, the daily interactions, and even your sense of who you are can seem a little uncertain. It's a shift that many find daunting, yet it's also a profound opportunity to rediscover yourself and redefine what makes you feel fulfilled. This chapter is about turning the page to that fresh chapter, where you redefine your purpose and engage with life in new and meaningful ways.

Let's start by exploring how you can reshape your identity post-retirement and find joy daily, filling what might initially feel like a void with activities and pursuits that resonate deeply with your core values and interests.

Redefining Purpose After the 9-to-5

The first days after retirement can often feel unsettling. You might wake up disoriented; the rhythm that once dictated your daily life is no longer there. It's not uncommon to experience a sense of loss or emptiness. Researchers and psychologists note that such feelings are normal; work provides structure, social interaction, and a sense of purpose. Dr. Robert Butler, a notable psychiatrist, emphasizes that retirement "is not merely a time of loss and decline, but also a time for growth and recognition."

Understanding this psychological impact is crucial. It helps you acknowledge these feelings without letting them define your retirement experience. To counteract these feelings, the first step is to reflect on your values and interests—many of which might have taken a backseat during your working years. Take a moment to write down activities or passions you used to love but haven't pursued in a while. Did you once enjoy painting? Were you an avid gardener, or did you love hiking through nature? Listing these can reignite old passions and inspire new pursuits.

Setting new goals is the next step, and it's something to approach with excitement rather than trepidation. Consider using the SMART (Specific, Measurable, Achievable, Relevant, Time-bound) goal framework tailored for retirees. For instance, if you wish to learn a new language, set a goal to learn 20 basic phrases in Spanish before your next family gathering or a trip to Spain. If volunteering strikes a chord, aim to identify and join a local community group within the next month. These goals give you direction and a sense of achievement as you tick them off individually.

Engaging in meaningful activities that align with these newly set goals can profoundly enhance your sense of purpose. Diverse options are available to fit different physical abilities and financial situations. For example, joining a walking group can offer exercise and social interaction, while crafting can be an excellent way to express creativity and even contribute handmade items to community centers. Activities like writing memoirs or engaging in online book clubs can be equally fulfilling for those with limited mobility.

Reflective Exercise

Take a moment to reflect on what values are most important to you now. Is it creativity, community, independence, or continuous learning? How can your activities align with these values? This reflection will help you live more intentionally and ensure your retirement is uniquely yours, filled with pursuits that bring joy and satisfaction.

By redefining your purpose after the 9-to-5 grind, embracing new and old passions, and setting achievable goals, you're not just filling time—you're building a rich life of joy and satisfaction.

Building a New Routine That Excites You

If there's one thing that often takes a backseat during our working years, it's the luxury of cultivating a daily routine that genuinely aligns with our joys and rhythms. Retirement opens up this unique space, a blank canvas if you will, where the structure of your day can be painted to suit your deepest desires and needs. It's not just about filling time; it's about enriching your life each day. Research consistently shows that having a structured daily routine can significantly boost mental health by reducing stress, enhancing sleep, and improving overall emotional well-being. Think of your routine as a gentle framework supporting your life, giving it shape and purpose while allowing enough flexibility to adapt.

Crafting a retirement-friendly daily schedule starts with understanding what you love and what keeps you energized. Begin by mapping out a typical week—pencil in fixed activities first, like meals, regular appointments, or commitments. Then, start weaving in activities that feed your soul. Mornings are perfect for indulging in hobbies like gardening or painting, where the quiet enhances your focus and creativity. Consider setting aside afternoons for physical activity—perhaps a walk in the park, swimming, or a yoga class. These keep you fit and boost your mood and energy levels.

Social interactions are vital, too; they keep us connected and grounded. Schedule regular meet-ups with friends and family, or volunteer your time in community activities. These engagements are invaluable; they provide a sense of belonging and purpose. And let's not forget downtime—essential for relaxation and reflection. Whether reading, listening to music, or simply napping, consciously allocate time to unwind and rejuvenate.

Flexibility in your routine is crucial. It's about finding a balance that accommodates days when you wake up brimming with energy, ready to tackle a new project or spontaneously decide to visit a new art exhibit or try out a new restaurant. Other days might call for quiet and solitude. The beauty of retirement is in this flexibility, the ability to listen to your body and mind and adjust accordingly. A helpful tip is to have a loose structure with blocks of time that can be easily shifted. Think of your routine as modular, where pieces can be moved as needed, but the overall picture still forms a harmonious whole.

Let's draw inspiration from others who've trodden this path. Take, for example, a friend of mine, John. He found his stride in retirement by setting a schedule that included volunteering at a local food bank twice a week, which gave him a profound sense of purpose and connection. He dedicates mornings to his long-time passion for woodworking, and afternoons are for leisurely walks or cycling with his wife. He's flexible with his evenings—sometimes hosting dinner parties and enjoying quiet nights. His routine isn't rigid, but it's a framework that keeps him engaged, balanced, and happy.

Creating a routine that excites you is about fully enjoying your retirement. It's not just about keeping busy; it's about doing things that bring joy, purpose, and wellness. It's about making sure each day is meaningful and fulfilling.

Overcoming the Initial Retirement Blues

The shift from a structured work life to the expansive retirement days can sometimes bring about an unexpected guest: the retirement blues. This emotional response can manifest as feelings of uselessness, persistent sadness, or even anxiety about what lies ahead. Recognizing these feelings is essential; they are common and manageable. Identifying these signs in yourself or others is the first step towards reclaiming joy and satisfaction in retirement.

Imagine waking up on a Monday morning with no office to go to, no meetings to prepare for, and no deadlines looming. While this might sound like a dream during the hectic work years, this new reality can feel unsettling once retirement sets in. You might find yourself lingering over the morning coffee longer than necessary, the television becoming a constant companion, or perhaps feelings of sadness creeping in with the afternoon's quiet. Such signs indicate retirement blues, signaling a need for new strategies to engage with life meaningfully.

Several approaches can be beneficial in managing these feelings. Mindfulness meditation, for instance, helps center your thoughts and calm your mind, teaching you to live in the present rather than worry about the past or future. This practice requires no special equipment or previous experience—simply a quiet space and a few minutes daily to focus on breathing and observe your thoughts without judgment. Journaling is another powerful tool. It allows you to express your thoughts and feelings on paper, which can help clarify your emotions and trigger insights and solutions. For those who find the blues lingering, seeking professional help from a counselor or therapist can provide the support needed to navigate this new phase of life effectively.

Social connections play a crucial role in combating feelings of isolation and depression, which often accompany the retirement blues. The key is to stay connected or even broaden your social network. You might start by joining clubs or groups that align with your interests. Whether it's a book club, a gardening group, or a cooking class, these gatherings provide regular social interaction and the opportunity to meet new people. Volunteering is another excellent way to stay connected. By contributing to your community, you not only enrich your own life but also make a meaningful difference in the lives of others. These activities provide structure to your days and a sense of accomplishment that is often missing in retirement.

Staying proactive in personal development is equally important. Retirement can be the perfect time to pursue education in a field you've always been interested in but never had the time to explore. Many universities and colleges offer courses for seniors, providing both an educational stimulus and a social environment. Part-time work or consulting in your professional field can also provide intellectual engagement and a sense of continuity from your previous career life. Such roles offer flexibility and a less demanding schedule while keeping you mentally active and integrated in a community.

Engaging in these strategies helps fill the void that retirement can sometimes bring. It transforms time that might otherwise be filled with loneliness or sadness into opportunities for growth, learning, and connection. The activities you engage in can reignite your sense of purpose and bring joy back into your daily life. Remember, the goal is not to replicate the busy schedule of your working years but to find a balance that keeps you connected to the world around you and true to your needs and interests.

As we adjust our sails to the breezes of retirement, we find that it's not merely about moving away from something; it's about moving toward something—a life of enrichment, engagement, and deep personal satisfaction. Each day brings the opportunity to explore, learn, and connect, gradually replacing the initial blues with a palette of brighter hues. Through proactive engagement and embracing new experiences, retirement can become a period of incredible transformation and joy.

TWO

Physical Wellness for the Golden Years

Imagine the gentle ebb and flow of the ocean waves, consistent and calming yet powerful in their reach. Like these waves, maintaining physical wellness as we age can be a soothing yet potent force, enhancing our day-to-day experiences and overall longevity. As we venture further into this chapter, think of your body as a vessel navigating these waters, where caring for it with the right exercises and practices isn't just about adding years to your life but life to your years.

Adaptable Exercises for Every Fitness Level

Creating an exercise routine that respects your body's current state and challenges its potential can be like crafting a personalized piece of art. It's about understanding and embracing your unique physical narrative, which includes those quirks brought on by years of living and moving. Whether you're dealing with arthritis, managing reduced mobility, or simply looking for ways to stay active, the goal is to tailor your physical activity so that it strengthens and revitalizes without overwhelming.

For many of us, the mention of exercise conjures images of heavy lifting or intense aerobic workouts. However, the beauty of fitness at this stage of life lies in its adaptability. Let's explore low-impact exercises that pack a punch in terms of benefits without the strain. Swimming, for instance, is a fantastic way to enhance cardiovascular health and maintain joint health. The buoyancy of water supports your body, reducing the risk of injury and pain that might come with other forms of exercise. Similarly, tai chi, often described as "meditation in motion," promotes deep breathing and slow, gentle movements that improve balance, flexibility, and calmness of mind. Yoga, too, can be modified for any fitness level, using props like chairs or yoga blocks to aid in poses, enhancing flexibility and muscle tone while also providing a stress-relieving mental workout.

Balance and coordination are crucial for preventing falls, a common concern as we age. Exercises that emphasize these skills are essential yet often overlooked. Simple routines such as standing on one leg or walking heel-to-toe can significantly improve your balance. Try gentle coordination exercises like tai chi or dance, which boost physical balance and enhance cognitive function by challenging your brain to learn new movement patterns.

In this digital age, technology offers many resources to guide your quest for a fit and healthy lifestyle. Numerous apps and online platforms provide a range of guided exercise routines designed specifically for seniors. These digital tools often feature videos demonstrating adaptations of standard exercises, ensuring your routine is safe, enjoyable, and effective. For instance, the app SilverSneakers GO, designed for seniors, offers workout programs that can be customized to your fitness level, complete with instructional videos that take you through each exercise step-by-step.

Interactive Element: Guided Exercise Routine

Try this simple balance exercise today:

- Stand near a stable surface (like a chair) that you can hold onto if needed.
- Lift your right foot off the ground and hold it there for as long as you can maintain balance, up to 30 seconds.
- Repeat with your left foot.
- Aim to do this exercise twice with each foot daily.

Adapting your exercise routine to fit your needs and conditions isn't just about staying physically active; it's about enhancing your quality of life, boosting your mood, and maintaining your independence. By choosing the right types of activities and using available tools and technology, you can create a balanced, enjoyable fitness regime that keeps you moving smoothly and steadily through your golden years, much like those serene, powerful ocean waves.

Nutrition Over 60: Eating Well for Longevity

As the seasons of life change, so too do our bodies, and with these changes come new needs and considerations—especially regarding nutrition. After all, food isn't just sustenance; it's medicine, comfort, and a cornerstone of maintaining vitality as we age. Adjusting our diets to meet the evolving needs of our bodies can significantly impact our energy levels, ability to fend off illnesses, and overall quality of life. Let's peel back the layers on how we can adapt our eating habits to nourish our bodies effectively in our golden years.

Our metabolic rate slows down with age, reducing the necessary calories. However, our requirements for certain nutrients increase, making it essential to choose foods that offer the biggest nutritional bang for each calorie consumed. For instance, calcium and vitamin D become crucial to help maintain bone health and mitigate the risk of osteoporosis. Foods rich in vitamin B12, like lean meats, fish, and dairy, are vital since the ability to absorb B12 decreases with age, and this vitamin is key for keeping blood and nerve cells healthy. Similarly, dietary fiber becomes paramount to aid digestive health and maintain regular bowel movements, which can be a concern in later years. A simple shift to integrate these needs is opting for fiber-rich whole grains, leafy greens, and fruits alongside sufficient protein sources low in saturated fats, such as fish or chicken.

Crafting meal plans that cater to these needs can be a smooth process. Consider the Mediterranean diet, often hailed for its balanced and heart-healthy approach, focusing on fruits, vegetables, whole grains, and healthy fats like olive oil, with moderate amounts of fish and poultry. This diet not only supports heart health but also aligns well with the nutritional needs of older adults. An example of a daily meal plan might include oatmeal topped with fresh berries and a sprinkle of flax seeds for breakfast, a grilled salmon salad with mixed greens, cherry tomatoes, and vinaigrette for lunch, and a dinner of chicken stir-fry loaded with a variety of colorful veggies over brown rice. Snacks could include yogurt with nuts or sliced apple with peanut butter, ensuring you're satisfied and receiving diverse nutrients throughout the day.

Hydration is another critical aspect often overlooked. As we age, our sense of thirst may diminish, increasing the risk of dehydration, which can exacerbate health issues and affect kidney function, cognition, and digestion. Consciously drinking fluids throughout the day is vital, and it doesn't always have to be water—soups, herbal teas, and water-rich fruits and vegetables also contribute to your daily fluid intake. Setting a reminder to sip water regularly or keeping a visible water pitcher nearby can be helpful strategies to stay hydrated.

Navigating dietary restrictions due to health conditions like diabetes, hypertension, or heart disease is another layer to consider. The good news is, with thoughtful adjustments, you can still enjoy a rich and varied diet. For those managing diabetes, balancing carbohydrate intake with whole, unprocessed foods can help maintain blood sugar levels. Incorporating heart-healthy foods that are low in sodium and high in potassium can aid in managing hypertension. Reading food labels becomes invaluable, allowing you to make informed choices about what goes into your cart and your body, avoiding hidden sugars, excessive sodium, and unhealthy fats.

Lastly, the role of supplements in a senior diet must be considered, although they should never replace a balanced diet. They can, however, complement your dietary intake, ensuring you receive all necessary nutrients. Before starting any new supplement regimen, a conversation with your healthcare provider is crucial to understand which supplements might benefit you based on your health needs and current medications. Common supplements for seniors include vitamin

D, vitamin B12, calcium, and omega-3 fatty acids, all supporting different aspects of health from bones to brain function.

Adjusting our diets as we age is about respecting our bodies' changing needs and responding with nourishment that sustains our physical health and zest for life.

The Importance of Regular Health Screenings

Navigating the intricacies of health screenings and preventative care might seem overwhelming, but consider these as proactive measures—much like servicing a car to keep it running smoothly. For us in our golden years, regular health check-ups and screenings are the tools that help maintain our engines, ensuring we can enjoy this phase of our lives without unwarranted health hiccups. Let's explore the particularly pivotal screenings for seniors and how to manage our health proactively through these measures.

Starting with health screenings tailored for seniors these are not just routine check-ups; they are crucial in catching potential health issues before they become serious problems. For instance, colonoscopies are recommended once every ten years starting at age 50, but if you have a family history of colorectal cancer, your doctor might suggest having them more frequently. Similarly, mammograms should be scheduled every one to two years for women starting at age 50, while men might be advised to have regular prostate exams. Bone density tests are also vital as they help detect osteoporosis early on, ensuring that preventive steps can be taken to protect your bone health. Each of these screenings has its recommended frequency, tailored to catch issues early and keep you active and healthy.

Managing multiple medications is another cornerstone of senior health. Many of us find ourselves juggling a variety of prescriptions that can be dizzying to manage. Regular reviews with your healthcare provider are essential to ensure that each medication is still necessary and that the combination of drugs isn't causing adverse interactions. This review can be as simple as conversing with your pharmacist or setting an appointment with your doctor to discuss your current medication regimen. It's about ensuring that each medication serves a purpose and that, collectively, they are not putting you at undue risk.

Preventative measures are your best defense against common health issues affecting seniors. Vaccinations play a crucial role here. The flu shot, for example, is an annual vaccine that you should consider, as it significantly reduces the risk of getting influenza, which can be severe at an older age. Pneumonia vaccines are recommended for all adults over 65, and the shingles vaccine is advised for those over 50. These vaccinations are crucial lines of defense, helping to prevent illnesses that can disrupt your life and lead to serious health complications.

Building a relationship with healthcare providers might not seem like a direct health measure, but it's incredibly impactful. Having a doctor who understands your health history, concerns, and lifestyle can significantly impact your overall health management. This relationship ensures that when issues arise, they are not viewed in isolation but in the context of your overall health and history. Being proactive in this relationship means preparing for appointments with questions or concerns about your health and being open about any symptoms or changes you've noticed. It's about creating a dialogue where your voice is heard, and your health priorities are addressed.

These proactive health measures—tailored screenings, effective medication management, preventative care, and a strong patient-provider relationship—are not just about avoiding diseases. They are about empowering you with the best strategies to enjoy your retirement fully, with health as a steadfast ally by your side.

As we wrap up this chapter on maintaining physical wellness, remember that the goal is to live vibrantly, not just longer. Regular health screenings, wise medication management, and preventative practices are key strategies that help pave the way for a healthy, fulfilling life in your later years. These measures ensure you survive and thrive, exploring this rich chapter of your life with confidence and good health.

In the next chapter, we'll continue exploring ways to enrich your retirement, focusing on emotional well-being and mental health. Just as we care for our bodies, nurturing our minds and spirits is equally essential for a harmonious and joyful retirement.

THREE

Cultivating Mental Sharpness

Imagine sitting in your favorite chair, perhaps with a warm cup of tea. The room is quiet and peaceful. Now, picture yourself reaching for a crossword puzzle or a Sudoku grid. As you focus on solving it, you're not just filling in boxes or connecting words; you're embarking on a mental workout that's as crucial as physical exercise. This chapter is dedicated to maintaining and enhancing your cognitive abilities through engaging, enjoyable brain games that promise to keep your mind as agile as a nimble chess piece dancing across the board.

Brain Games That Boost Mental Flexibility

When we think of staying fit, our minds usually go straight to physical activities, but mental fitness is equally important. Brain games, which include a variety of puzzles, memory games, and problem-solving activities, serve as the weights and treadmills for your mind. These games help improve cognitive functions by challenging your ability to think critically, solve problems, and remember details. For instance, engaging with a Sudoku puzzle enhances logical thinking and concentration, while solving crosswords can expand your vocabulary and general knowledge. These activities stimulate neural pathways, helping maintain and improve cognitive agility as you age.

Selecting the right brain games can be like choosing the perfect book; it must align with your interests to keep you engaged. For instance, if you're a history buff, you might enjoy trivia quizzes that challenge your knowledge of historical events. If you love language, crosswords or word searches could be your go-to. The key is to find games you enjoy because the more you enjoy the activity, the more likely you will stick with it regularly. Numerous online and offline resources are available to help you find games that suit your preferences. Websites like Lumosity offer personalized brain training programs that adjust to your performance and preferences, providing a continuous challenge. Offline, simple puzzle books can be found in most bookstores, offering a portable and inexpensive way to keep your mind engaged.

Incorporating these brain games into your daily routine is crucial. As you might set aside time for physical exercise, dedicating specific times for mental workouts can help you maintain a balanced schedule. It doesn't have to be lengthy; even 15 to 20 minutes daily can significantly impact the process. Try starting your morning with a puzzle or unwinding in the evening with a solitaire game or a few pages of riddles. Consistency will improve your cognitive abilities and provide a structured break where you can mentally regroup and relax.

Staying motivated can sometimes take time, especially if progress seems slow. Setting small, achievable goals within these games can provide a sense of accomplishment and encourage you to keep pushing forward. For example, if you're working on a particularly challenging crossword puzzle, you might aim to complete at least three clues daily. Tracking your progress can also be motivating. Keep a simple log of the games you do and note any improvements—maybe you solve the puzzles faster or remember more details than before. Celebrate these small victories; they are signs of your brain growing stronger. Regularly adding new types of games or increasing the difficulty level can keep the challenge fresh and prevent you from hitting a plateau.

Interactive Element: Brain Flex Challenge

Try this fun exercise to see how quickly you can think on your feet:

- Find a partner or a timer.
- Choose a category (e.g., fruits, countries, book titles).
- Set a timer for 2 minutes.
- Name as many items as possible from that category until the timer runs out.
- Record your total and try to beat your score next time!

Involving friends or family in these activities can also turn brain training into a social event, adding to the enjoyment and benefits. Whether competing in trivia nights, playing strategy games like chess or bridge, or solving puzzles together, these shared activities can enhance your social bonds while sharpening everyone's cognitive skills.

Lifelong Learning: Opportunities and Resources

There's something truly exhilarating about discovering a new interest or delving deeper into a beloved subject. This thrill, my friends, isn't just for the young; it's a lifelong gift, and as retirees, we are in a prime position to unwrap it daily. Embracing continuous learning sharpens the mind and enriches the soul, offering a robust defense against the mental rust that sometimes accompanies aging. Research consistently shows that seniors who engage in educational activities can significantly reduce their risks of cognitive decline. A study by the American Academy of Neurology suggests that individuals who actively learn new skills lower their chances of developing memory problems or dementia.

Accessing learning opportunities nowadays is easier than ever, and you only have to leave the comfort of your home if you want to. Many local community colleges offer courses tailored for seniors, providing a range of subjects from computer skills to art history. These classes are often discounted for older adults, making them an affordable way to stay intellectually active. The internet is a treasure trove of knowledge for those who prefer learning from home. Platforms like Coursera and Udemy feature courses taught by university professors and industry experts from around the globe. Whether you want to explore the mysteries of ancient civilizations, understand the basics of photography, or even dip your toes into modern technology, these sites have you covered.

Diving into diverse subjects broadens your knowledge and plays a pivotal role in maintaining mental health. Learning new skills can be incredibly fulfilling, injecting excitement and variety into your daily routine. It challenges your brain in new ways, keeps your neurons firing, and increases your sense of self-efficacy. Moreover, the joy of mastering a new skill or understanding a complex topic can significantly boost your mood and overall outlook on life. Imagine the satisfaction of finally figuring out how to use that software your grandchildren are always chatting about or being able to discuss the latest bestseller in depth at your next book club meeting.

The social aspect of learning is just as important as the intellectual benefits. Creating or joining a learning community can enhance this experience tremendously. Consider forming a study group with fellow learners; this can be an informal gathering where each member shares insights from their learning adventures, or you might collectively tackle a course or a challenging book. Attending lectures or talks as a group is another fantastic way to foster community connections while expanding your knowledge base. These gatherings can turn learning into a social event, providing intellectual stimulation and valuable social interaction essential for emotional well-being.

Engaging with various subjects, embracing new learning platforms, and participating in educational communities keep your mind sharp and enrich your retirement with continuous growth and joyous discovery. So, why not start today? Pick a topic you've always been curious about and take the first step on what promises to be an enlightening path. After all, every day holds the potential to be a learning day; every lesson learned is a step towards a more fulfilling life.

The Benefits of Routine Mental Health Check-Ins

Navigating the emotional landscape of retirement can sometimes feel like trying to steer a boat through uncharted waters. It's not uncommon to encounter waves of depression, anxiety, or isolation, which can cloud our days and impact our cognitive functions and overall zest for life. Recognizing these challenges is the first step toward maintaining your mental health and enhancing your overall quality of life during these golden years.

Depression and anxiety can often be more difficult to identify in one's later years, as they might be mistakenly attributed to age-related changes or physical health issues. Signs to watch out for include persistent sadness, loss of interest in previously enjoyed activities, withdrawal from social interactions, or excessive worrying. Similarly, feelings of isolation can creep in as life's circumstances change, such as losing a spouse, friends moving away, or physical limitations that reduce mobility. These feelings can lead to a significant decline in mental and emotional well-being if not addressed. Understanding that these are common experiences among many seniors can help you feel less alone and more empowered to seek solutions.

Implementing regular mental health self-assessments is a proactive strategy that can make a tremendous difference. Think of these check-ins as routine maintenance for your mind, helping ensure that minor issues can be addressed before they become more significant problems. You can conduct these assessments by regularly asking yourself questions about your mood, thoughts, and overall emotional state. For instance, have you been feeling more irritable or down than usual? Are you finding it harder to get motivated? If you notice changes that concern you, it's important not to dismiss them. Documenting these observations can be helpful when discussing them with a healthcare provider, giving a clearer picture of your mental health over time.

The role of professional mental health services in retirement cannot be overstated. Counseling and therapy can provide essential support, offering strategies to manage stress, cope with loss, and reframe negative thinking that might lead to depression or anxiety. These services also play a crucial role in maintaining cognitive health, as unaddressed mental health issues can exacerbate cognitive decline. Many communities offer mental health services tailored specifically for seniors, recognizing the unique challenges faced during this life stage. Whether through individual counseling sessions or group therapy, engaging with these services can provide valuable insights, tools, and reassurance that you are not navigating these challenges alone.

Incorporating daily practices that support mental wellness is equally vital. Meditation, journaling, and mindfulness can significantly enhance your mental health routine. Meditation, for instance, helps center your thoughts and calm your mind, serving as a reset button for your emotional state. It can reduce stress, enhance your mood, and improve sleep quality—all essential for cognitive health and general well-being. Journaling, on the other hand, offers a way to express your thoughts and feelings, which can be particularly therapeutic if you're grappling with loss or transition. It provides a private space to confront and make sense of your emotions, fostering a deeper understanding of yourself and your mental health. Mindfulness, or being present and fully engaged with the moment, can transform simple daily activities into profound mental engagement and relaxation opportunities.

Each of these practices is part of your overall mental health care. Integrating them into your daily routine can help you manage the stresses of life, enhance your cognitive functions, and maintain a connection to your own experiences and emotions. By regularly checking in with yourself, engaging in professional mental health services when necessary, and practicing daily wellness routines, you are setting yourself up not just for a retirement that is survivable but one that is richly enjoyable.

As we close this chapter on enhancing mental sharpness and emotional well-being, let us understand that mental health is as crucial to our quality of life as physical health. Looking ahead, the next chapter will explore the deep interconnections between emotional well-being and the relationships we cherish, guiding you through nurturing these connections to enhance your retirement life.

FOUR

Emotional Well-Being in Retirement

As the golden hues of sunset paint the sky, marking the end of another day, it's a poignant reminder that each phase of life, too, transitions into another. Retirement, with its wealth of free time and opportunities, can also bring significant emotional shifts, including the experience of grief and loss. These feelings aren't reserved just for the loss of loved ones but can also encompass the loss of one's identity, purpose, or even physical abilities that once defined daily life. In this chapter, we'll explore these sensitive areas, offering guidance and strategies to cope with these losses and find pathways that lead from mourning to meaningful personal growth.

Handling Grief and Loss in Later Life

Grief in retirement can often feel like an uninvited guest who doesn't want to leave. It's multifaceted: sorrow from losing a spouse or a close friend, the stark realization of physical limitations that modify lifestyle choices, or the profound sense of loss when the daily routines of a decades-long career come to an end. Each loss carries its weight, impacting emotional well-being and necessitating adjustment and healing.

One of the most effective ways to cope with grief is through community support—people who understand and share the unique challenges of grieving in later life. Many communities and online platforms offer support groups specifically tailored for seniors dealing with loss. These groups provide a safe space to express feelings, share experiences, and learn from others navigating similar challenges. Engaging in these groups can help alleviate the isolation often accompanying grief, reminding you that you are not alone in your experiences.

Another powerful tool in the journey through grief is engagement in therapeutic activities. Writing, for instance, can be a profound way of processing emotions. Keeping a journal where you can express your thoughts and feelings daily helps manage the intensity of grief, providing a private space to confront and understand your emotions. Art, whether painting, sculpture, or another form, also offers a therapeutic outlet. It allows for expressing grief in a manner that words sometimes cannot capture, helping to process complex emotions through creativity.

The importance of ritual in the grieving process cannot be understated. Rituals, whether formal or informal, public or private, help acknowledge loss and offer ways to commemorate and honor those no longer with us. This could be something as simple as lighting a candle daily at a specific time to remember a loved one, participating in a community memorial event, or creating a small garden or artwork as a tribute. These rituals structure the grieving process, offering tangible ways to express sorrow while also celebrating the memory of loved ones.

Transitioning from grief to growth involves finding new meanings and joys in life that can gradually replace the pain of loss. Volunteering offers a pathway out of grief by shifting focus from self to others. Engaging in activities that help others can provide a sense of purpose and fulfillment that your loss might have diminished. Similarly, mentoring others in your field of expertise or in hobbies you are passionate about can bring a renewed sense of identity and purpose. Adopting new hobbies that challenge you physically and mentally can also refocus your energy positively, helping to cultivate a sense of achievement and self-worth.

Reflective Exercise: Journaling Prompt

Consider starting a grief journal. Write about your feelings and memories of your loved ones each day, or express anything. Over time, review your entries to observe how your feelings have evolved. This can be a private way to monitor your healing process and remind you of your strength to overcome difficult times.

In navigating the complexities of grief in retirement, remember that it's a deeply personal experience—no two paths through it are exactly the same. By seeking support, engaging in therapeutic activities, honoring loved ones with rituals, and finding new avenues for personal growth, you can manage the impact of loss and move towards a renewed sense of purpose and joy in your life.

Cultivating Gratitude and Positivity

Each moment of gratitude we embrace adds strength and color, turning everyday experiences into a rich mosaic of memories and joys. Research, particularly focusing on seniors, underscores how cultivating a sense of gratitude can significantly enhance mental health, leading to greater life satisfaction and reduced stress. Studies from leading institutions have shown that gratitude improves your psychological health by reducing toxic emotions like envy and resentment and fosters resilience, enabling you to bounce back more quickly from challenging situations. For seniors, this practice can be especially transformative, turning the golden years into a time of growth and positivity.

One practical way to cultivate gratitude is by keeping a gratitude journal, a simple yet profoundly effective tool for fostering appreciation daily. Start by setting aside a few minutes daily to write down three things you are grateful for. These don't have to be grand events; even small, everyday occurrences like a pleasant conversation, a good cup of coffee, or the sun's warmth can be worthy of gratitude. Writing them downshifts your focus from what's missing or problematic to what's abundant and right in your life, gradually altering your perspective and enhancing your overall contentment.

Engaging in daily reflection practices is another cornerstone of building gratitude. This could be a quiet moment each morning where you reflect on what you're looking forward to or a nightly reflection on what went well during the day. Mindfulness practices can bolster these reflections, which root you in the present moment, helping you appreciate your current experiences more deeply. Mindfulness can be as simple as paying full attention to a routine task, listening intently to a friend without planning your next words, or savoring a meal by fully experiencing its flavors and textures. This attentiveness to the present heightens your appreciation of life and dilutes worries about the past and anxieties about the future, fostering a tranquil mind.

Expressing gratitude to others is equally important. This could be verbally thanking someone for a small kindness, writing a thoughtful note, or even sharing a positive post on social media acknowledging someone's impact on your life. These acts of acknowledgment strengthen your relationships and create a positive feedback loop, enhancing your happiness. You see, gratitude is contagious; it not only lifts your spirits but also those of everyone around you, creating a community of positivity and support.

Celebrating small victories is vital in maintaining a positive outlook, especially in retirement when major career milestones might no longer define your achievements. These mini-celebrations can be as simple as acknowledging the completion of a daily crossword puzzle, successfully adding a new recipe to your culinary repertoire, or the ability to help a friend with a challenging task. Each small victory is a reaffirmation of your capabilities and boosts your self-esteem. It can be particularly empowering during a phase of life when societal narratives sometimes lean towards what seniors can't do rather than celebrating what they can.

Integrating these practices into your daily life doesn't require monumental changes but small, consistent gestures of gratitude and mindfulness. Over time, these small steps can significantly shift your outlook, transforming the landscape of your retirement into one marked by joy, gratitude, and positivity. As you continue to cultivate these habits, you'll find that you are living more joyously and creating a ripple effect, enriching the lives of those around you with your renewed energy and perspective.

Solo but Not Lonely: Thriving in Solitude

Embracing solitude, especially in retirement, doesn't have to equate to loneliness. Solitude can be deeply enriching and peaceful when approached with the right mindset. It allows for self-reflection, creativity, and personal growth. However, it's crucial to distinguish it from loneliness, which often carries feelings of isolation and disconnection. While solitude is a chosen state of being alone and can lead to self-discovery and tranquility, loneliness is an imposed state that can lead to sadness and separation from others. Understanding and embracing the positive aspects of solitude can transform it into a powerful ally during your retirement years.

Solitude offers the perfect backdrop for engaging in activities that nurture your soul and spark your creativity. For instance, meditation can be a profound practice during solitary moments, allowing you to delve deep into your thoughts and emotions, leading to greater self-awareness and peace. Similarly, taking walks in nature not only provides the physical benefits of exercise but also the mental benefits of being in a calming environment, which can enhance your mood and overall sense of well-being. Reading is another activity that flourishes in solitude; it allows you to explore new worlds, ideas, and perspectives at your own pace, enriching your knowledge and experience.

Solo hobbies also play a crucial role in making the most of your solitude. Painting, writing, gardening, or even cooking special meals for yourself can be incredibly fulfilling. These activities keep you physically and mentally active and allow you to express yourself creatively, which can be especially rewarding. The key is choosing hobbies you enjoy, challenging yourself, keeping your mind engaged, and sharpening your skills.

Building self-reliance and confidence in retirement is another significant aspect of thriving in solitude. Setting personal challenges and learning new skills independently can greatly enhance your competence and self-assurance. Whether learning to use new technology, mastering a new art technique, or even studying a new subject area, each new skill you acquire builds your confidence and enriches your life. These achievements remind you of your capabilities and resilience, boosting your self-esteem and encouraging you to continue exploring and growing.

While solitude has many benefits, maintaining a balance with social interaction is essential to prevent it from slipping into loneliness. Regular communication with family and friends, whether through phone calls, texts, or social media, helps keep you connected with your loved community. Planning regular outings or visits with friends and family can also provide the necessary social interaction and strengthen your relationships, ensuring that while you enjoy solitude, you are not isolated from the world.

Navigating the delicate balance between enjoying solitude and avoiding loneliness involves embracing alone time as an opportunity for growth and reflection while ensuring you remain actively connected to your community and loved ones.

By finding joy and fulfillment in solitary activities and maintaining strong social connections, you can enjoy the best of both worlds—using solitude to enrich your personal life and social interactions to enhance your emotional well-being.

As we reflect on the insights shared in this chapter about the emotional dimensions of retirement—from handling grief and loss to cultivating gratitude and positivity and thriving in solitude—we see a collection of strategies to help manage the emotional transitions of this life phase. These strategies are about coping and thriving, turning potential challenges into opportunities for growth and fulfillment.

Looking ahead to the next chapter, we will explore how maintaining physical health and wellness plays a pivotal role in supporting a vibrant and fulfilling retirement. Just as we nurture our emotional well-being, taking care of our physical health provides a strong foundation for enjoying all that retirement has to offer.

FIVE

Financial Security Without Compromise

Imagine a calm, clear morning with endless possibilities. This is what your retirement can be—clear, calm, and financially stable. But getting there can be tricky, especially when it comes to money. This chapter will help you make smart financial decisions to ensure your retirement is stress-free and secure.

Smart Budgeting for Fixed Incomes

When managing finances in retirement, understanding your financial flow—the ins and outs of your income and expenses—is crucial. It's like understanding the rhythm of the tides when sailing; you need to know when to set sail and when to anchor down. Keeping a detailed record of where your money comes from and where it goes is the first step in navigating these waters. Tools and apps like Mint or PocketGuard can be invaluable here, offering a clear overview and real-time tracking of your finances. These tools categorize your spending automatically, helping you see how much you spend on necessities like groceries, utilities, and health versus what you're splurging on, say, dining out or hobbies.

Creating a sustainable budget on a fixed income is much like planning a well-balanced diet—it should be nutritious enough to maintain good health (in this case, financial health) and flexible enough to allow for the occasional treat. List your fixed expenses, such as housing, utilities, and insurance. Then, factor in regular costs like food, transportation, and medical expenses. What's left can be allocated to discretionary spending—those little pleasures that brighten your day. Remember, balance is key; overspending in one area might mean tightening the belt in another. However, life is unpredictable, and financial situations can change—prices can increase, and unexpected expenses can arise. Your budget should be revisited and adjusted regularly to reflect these changes, ensuring it always meets your current needs.

Cutting unnecessary expenses doesn't mean cutting out joy. It's about making smarter choices that stretch your dollars further. For instance, examine your utility bills; could you save by switching to a different provider or using energy more efficiently? Cable bills can often be reduced by canceling channels you never watch or, increasingly, by cutting the cable cord altogether in favor of cheaper streaming services. Subscriptions and memberships should also be evaluated—are you using that gym membership, or could those walks or yoga sessions at home serve you just as well? Being mindful of these choices can lead to significant savings without diminishing your quality of life.

Lastly, ensure you're taking full advantage of discounts and benefits available to seniors. Many retailers, service providers, and even utility companies offer discounts to older adults. Additionally, government programs and community-sponsored benefits can provide financial relief or assistance in health care, utilities, and property taxes. Organizations like AARP offer a wealth of resources on available senior discounts and benefits, which can help reduce your expenses significantly.

Interactive Element: Budget Review Exercise

Grab a notebook or open a spreadsheet, and start tracking your monthly expenses. Categorize them as 'Necessary' or 'Discretionary.' At the end of the month, review your spending. Are there subscriptions or services you didn't use? Is there a recurring expense that surprised you? Use this insight to adjust your budget for the next month, aiming to reduce unnecessary expenditures.

By mastering the art of budgeting on a fixed income, utilizing tools to track financial flow, creating a balanced and flexible budget, cutting unnecessary expenses, and maximizing discounts and benefits, you can secure your financial stability without compromising the quality and enjoyment of your retirement life. This proactive approach ensures that your finances are well-managed and provides peace of mind, allowing you to focus more on enjoying your retirement and less on worrying about money.

Planning for Unexpected Health Costs

Navigating the waters of healthcare expenses in retirement can often feel like trying to steer through a fog—uncertain and a bit unpredictable. Yet, with thoughtful planning and strategic foresight, you can clear the mist and ensure that unexpected health costs do not disrupt your peaceful retirement life. Understanding the typical health-related costs you might encounter is a crucial first step. These costs can range widely, from regular medications and ongoing treatments for chronic conditions to more sudden expenses such as emergency medical procedures or the need for specialized care. Even with Medicare, out-of-pocket costs can include deductibles, copays, and coinsurance, which can add up quickly and significantly impact your budget.

Building an emergency health fund is your safety net. It's about preparing for the unexpected to ensure such expenses don't derail your financial stability. Start by reviewing your current health expenses to understand what you might need in the future. Consider how these might increase with age and factor in the potential for unforeseen conditions or treatments. A general rule of thumb is to set aside enough funds to cover your out-of-pocket maximum for at least one year. This amount should be kept in a readily accessible account, such as a high-yield savings account or a money market account, where the balance can grow but remains available without penalties should you need it suddenly.

Insurance plays a pivotal role in managing health-related expenses, acting like a buoy that helps keep you afloat during high tides. Navigating Medicare, supplemental policies, or private health insurance options can be complex, but understanding what your policies cover and what gaps you might need to fill is essential. Regularly review your health insurance policies to ensure they match your current health needs, which can change as you age. For instance, if you develop a chronic condition requiring frequent specialist visits or expensive medication, ensuring your policy covers these can save you significant money. Additionally, suppose your current policy premiums or out-of-pocket costs become too burdensome. In that case, it might be time to shop for a new plan offering better coverage or more suitable terms.

Navigating government aid and subsidies can significantly alleviate the burden of healthcare costs. Many seniors need to be aware of all the available benefits, including assistance with prescription drugs, medical devices, and even some preventive services. Programs like Medicaid can provide coverage if your income falls below a certain level, and the Extra Help program can assist with Medicare prescription drug plan costs. Each program has specific eligibility criteria, which can sometimes be confusing, but taking the time to understand these can result in substantial savings. Local senior centers, health care providers, and specific online resources can guide and assist in applying for these programs, ensuring you receive every benefit you're entitled to.

Managing healthcare costs in retirement can be a manageable task. With a clear understanding of potential expenses, a well-funded emergency health account, carefully chosen insurance coverage, and an awareness of available government aid, you can secure your financial health against unexpected medical costs. This proactive approach allows you to enjoy your retirement with one less worry, confident that you are well-prepared to handle whatever health issues come your way.

Investment Tips for the Risk-Averse Retiree

Navigating the investment landscape in your golden years can seem like a delicate balancing act. You want to ensure your money works for you, bringing in sufficient income to cover your lifestyle without exposing you to undue risk. Let's explore some investment options well-suited to those who prefer to stay on the safer side of the investment spectrum, focusing on stability and steady income.

Bonds, fixed annuities, and dividend-paying stocks are three pillars of low-risk investment strategies that can offer you peace of mind and financial stability. Bonds, essentially loans to the government or corporations that pay you interest over a set period, are traditionally considered safe investments. The risk associated with bonds correlates with the issuer's creditworthiness; Treasury bonds issued by the U.S. government, for instance, are very secure, while corporate bonds can vary in risk based on the company's financial health.

Fixed annuities, another conservative investment option, provide a guaranteed income over some time. You pay a lump sum upfront, and the insurance company promises to pay you a set amount periodically. This can be particularly appealing if you're looking for predictable income streams. However, it's crucial to consider the fees associated with annuities and the insurance company's financial strength.

Dividend-paying stocks offer a share in a company's profits and typically attract investors looking for steady income and potential stock value increases. Companies that regularly pay dividends are more established and financially stable, which can provide some reassurance if the market fluctuates. However, it's important to remember that stocks can never be entirely risk-free and fluctuate with market changes.

Diversifying your investment portfolio is like putting only some eggs in one basket. A well-balanced portfolio can help protect against market volatility and safeguard your investments from the unexpected twists and turns of the economy. For instance, mixing bonds with dividend-paying stocks can balance the potential risks and returns. Additionally, incorporating some real estate funds or commodities like gold can further diversify your investments, potentially reducing risk and improving returns over time.

Setting realistic investment goals is crucial. At this stage in life, your focus might be more on preserving capital and generating consistent income rather than achieving high returns, which typically involve higher risks. Consider your current financial situation, expenses, and how much risk you can tolerate. For example, if your primary goal is to fund your everyday living expenses, you might prioritize investments that offer stability and regular income over those with higher growth potential but greater risk.

Seeking professional financial advice can be incredibly beneficial, especially if you want to become more experienced in investing. A trustworthy financial advisor can provide personalized advice based on your financial situation, risk tolerance, and retirement goals. They can help you understand the complex world of investments, assist in building and maintaining a diversified portfolio, and plan for long-term financial security. When choosing a financial advisor, look for someone with a solid track of ethical standards and performance. Check their credentials, ask for references, and ensure they understand your financial goals and personal circumstances.

As we wrap up this discussion on investments, remember that the key to successful investing in retirement is not just about choosing the right assets but managing them in a way that aligns with your overall financial goals and risk tolerance. By focusing on low-risk investments, diversifying your portfolio, setting realistic goals, and seeking professional advice, you can enjoy a financially secure retirement that lets you live comfortably and with peace of mind.

Looking ahead, we will explore ways to stay socially connected and active, which is important for your emotional and mental well-being and can also profoundly impact your physical health. Just as we manage our finances to ensure stability, maintaining our social networks ensures a rich, fulfilling life full of joy and community engagement.

SIX

Staying Socially Connected

Imagine stepping into a garden vibrant with colors and alive with the buzz of community—the laughter of friends, the shared whispers between neighbors, the clinking of coffee cups. This image, rich with connection and warmth, illustrates what staying socially connected in retirement could look like. Often, as we transition away from the structured social environments of our working lives, the question arises: how do we continue to cultivate these enriching social landscapes? The answer lies in embracing new engagement opportunities, such as joining clubs and groups that align with our interests and passions.

Joining Clubs and Groups: A Gateway to New Friendships

The beauty of retirement is the gift of time—time to dive into interests that you may have only skimmed the surface of during your busier working days. Now, you can immerse yourself fully, perhaps in literary discussions at a book club or getting your hands dirty in the tranquility of a community garden. These interest-based clubs are not just about indulging in your passions but also vibrant avenues for meeting others who share your interests.

Finding the right group might initially seem daunting, but the process can be quite delightful. Start by listing what you love doing or what you've always wanted to explore. Once you have your list, check out local community boards, libraries, and online platforms like Meetup.com. These resources are treasure troves of information on existing groups in your area. Libraries, in particular, often host various events and clubs—from book discussions to knitting circles—and can give you a gentle introduction to these groups.

The benefits of regular meetups with these groups extend far beyond learning a new gardening technique or discussing a novel. They forge connections, build friendships, and create a sense of belonging crucial for emotional well-being. Psychologically, being part of a group can significantly diminish feelings of loneliness and isolation—a common challenge in retirement. Furthermore, these interactions stimulate the mind and can keep you mentally sharp. Engaging in regular, meaningful conversations with others will not only enrich your social life but also enhance your mental resilience.

Perhaps you've noticed a gap—a club or group that doesn't yet exist in your community but should. Starting your group can be incredibly rewarding and is not as intimidating as it might seem. Begin by defining the purpose of your group: Is it social, educational, recreational, or a mix? Once you have a clear vision, recruit members by reaching out through community bulletin boards, social media platforms, and local community centers. When setting up meetings, consider accessibility for all members regarding location, time, and physical accessibility. Managing a group effectively requires clear communication, so establishing regular schedules and keeping everyone informed is key. Remember, the goal is to create a welcoming and inclusive environment where all members feel valued and engaged.

Navigating group dynamics can be challenging, but it's essential for maintaining a healthy and enjoyable environment. Set basic ground rules for discussions and interactions to ensure all members feel heard and respected. Conflicts may arise but can be managed through open and respectful communication. Sometimes, acknowledging different viewpoints and finding common ground can resolve issues. The aim is to foster a supportive community where everyone can thrive.

Exploring new clubs and groups in retirement is much like gardening. It starts with planting seeds—in this case, ideas and interests—and nurturing them through regular engagement and care. Over time, these seeds grow into flourishing gardens of friendship and community, transforming your retirement into a vibrant landscape of joyful connections.

Interactive Element: Reflection Section

Take a moment to reflect on your interests and passions. What activities make you lose track of time? Consider how you share these passions with others. Could you join a club or start one? Jot down a few ideas on engaging more deeply with these interests through social groups or clubs. This exercise is not just about filling your calendar; it's about enriching your social world and enhancing your overall quality of life in retirement.

Volunteering: Socialize While Giving Back

Volunteering can enrich your life immensely, offering a unique blend of social engagement and the deep satisfaction of contributing to your community. When considering volunteer opportunities, selecting activities that resonate with your interests and leveraging your strengths is essential, ensuring that your time spent volunteering is enjoyable and impactful. Begin by assessing your passion—education, animal welfare, health care, or the arts. This reflection helps ensure that the work you choose is meaningful to you and keeps you engaged over time.

Finding the right opportunity can be as straightforward as visiting volunteer matching websites such as VolunteerMatch.org or Idealist.org. These platforms allow you to search for opportunities based on your interests, skills, and the amount of time you can commit. They can also help you find roles that are specifically seeking senior volunteers, recognizing the valuable experience and perspective that you bring. Before committing, consider how much time you can realistically dedicate to volunteering. It's important to choose a commitment that fits comfortably into your life without overwhelming you, allowing you to enjoy both the work and your leisure time.

The social benefits of volunteering are vast and can significantly enhance your sense of connectivity. As you engage with various projects, you'll meet people from all walks of life, each with different stories and backgrounds. This diversity enriches your experience and broadens your understanding of the community around you. Volunteering also often leads to new friendships and strengthens your ties to the community, providing a network of support and camaraderie. Regular interactions with fellow volunteers and community members can help alleviate feelings of loneliness and isolation, which are common retirement concerns.

Volunteering is wider than one type of activity or setting, and many environments thrive on the participation of senior volunteers. For example, schools often welcome retirees who can help with tutoring, reading programs, or after-school activities, providing students with valuable educational support and mentorship. Hospitals and healthcare facilities also offer a range of volunteer positions, from assisting in patient care to administrative duties or supporting family members of patients. Nonprofit organizations, particularly those focused on seniors, hunger relief, housing, and community development, also provide numerous meaningful opportunities to contribute. In these roles, you can see the direct impact of your efforts on the community, which can be incredibly rewarding.

For those looking for a deeper level of engagement, long-term volunteer commitments can be especially fulfilling. Taking on a role such as a project coordinator or a leadership position within a volunteer organization can provide a sense of purpose and continuity. These roles allow you to build and lead projects, manage teams, and see initiatives from conception to completion. They can be challenging but immensely rewarding, offering a chance to use your professional skills and life experience in new and impactful ways. Long-term volunteering fosters a strong sense of belonging and achievement as you become integral to the organization's mission and growth.

Volunteering offers a pathway to stay socially active and mentally engaged, all while contributing to the betterment of your community. It allows you to learn new skills, connect with others, and, most importantly, make a significant impact on the lives of others. Whether volunteering a few hours a week or taking on a more substantial role, your contributions are valuable and appreciated. As you step into any of these roles, you'll find that giving back not only helps others—it enriches your life, bringing joy and fulfillment in ways that few other activities can.

Using Technology to Stay in Touch

In today's digital age, staying connected with loved ones and the world around you has never been more accessible or more enriching. Embracing technology can transform how you interact and maintain relationships, especially if physical distances keep you apart from friends and family. Whether checking in on grandchildren via video calls or catching up with old friends through social media, the digital tools available today can significantly enhance your social life and help you stay connected.

Video calling apps like Skype and Zoom have revolutionized communication, allowing us to see and speak with others as if they were in the same room. These platforms are user-friendly and can be a fantastic way to keep in touch with family and friends. Setting up these apps might initially seem daunting, but the process is quite straightforward. Begin by downloading the app on your smartphone, tablet, or computer. Create an account, usually requiring only an email address and a password. Once set up, you can instantly connect with others by searching for their contact information or sending an invitation to connect. It's essential to familiarize yourself with the privacy settings on these platforms, ensuring that your communications are secure and that you're comfortable with who can contact you.

Instant messaging apps such as WhatsApp and Facebook Messenger offer another layer of connectivity, allowing for real-time text conversations, sharing photos, or even sending voice messages. These tools are excellent for quick check-ins or sharing spontaneous moments throughout your day. Social media platforms like Facebook and Instagram also offer an excellent way to stay updated on the lives of those you care about and share updates about your own life. You can post photos, share thoughts, and even join groups of like-minded individuals who share your hobbies or interests.

Online communities and forums can be a treasure trove of connection and information, particularly if your physical mobility is limited or you live in a remote area. Many websites host forums that unite people based on shared interests such as gardening, books, cars, health, or even retirement living. Engaging in these forums can provide social interaction, valuable information, and support from others who share your interests or experiences. Websites like Reddit or specialized forums related to your hobbies can be accessed quickly and often have specific sections dedicated to senior users.

Maintaining relationships from a distance has always been challenging, thanks to these technological advances. Regular video calls can help you stay involved in the lives of your family members, watch grandchildren grow up, or celebrate milestones in real time despite the miles. Sharing photos and updates via social media or instant messaging keeps daily communication lively and engaging. For family events like birthdays or holidays, organizing a group video call can make you feel right in the heart of the festivities, even if you're celebrating from afar.

Therefore, technology bridges the gap caused by physical distance and enriches your daily interactions, making them more frequent and meaningful. It ensures that you remain an integral part of your loved ones' lives, sharing their joys and offering support during challenging times, all with just a few clicks.

As we wrap up this exploration of how technology can keep you socially connected, it's clear that these digital tools are not just conveniences but essential elements that enrich your social interactions and help maintain your relationships. They allow you to stay actively engaged with your community, family, and friends, enhancing the quality of your life and ensuring you never feel disconnected.

The next chapter will discuss another crucial aspect of a fulfilling retirement: embracing lifelong learning. We'll explore how continuing to learn and grow can enrich your life, offering new challenges and opportunities to engage with the world around you.

SEVEN

Technology and the Modern Senior

I magine yourself in a cozy armchair, a cup of tea by your side, embarking on a voyage not across the seas but into the digital world, equipped with gadgets that might once have seemed like the stuff of science fiction. Technology, which evolves quicker than any other, offers tools and devices that can significantly enhance daily life, especially in retirement. While the rapid pace of technological advancement can sometimes feel daunting, embracing this can lead to greater independence, safety, and a richer connection with the world around you.

Essential Tech for Everyday Use

The array of smart devices available today—smartphones, tablets, and home automation tools—can be incredibly beneficial. These devices are designed to make life easier, safer, and more enjoyable, offering useful functionalities for seniors. Let's start by demystifying some of these technological wonders and explore how they can fit seamlessly into your daily life.

Smartphones and tablets, for instance, are much more than devices for making calls or sending messages. They are compact computers that keep you connected with family, manage your appointments, and even monitor your health. Certain features make particular models more user-friendly for those of us in the golden years. For example, smartphones with voice command capabilities allow you to operate the device without fumbling for glasses to see tiny icons. You can simply send messages, make calls, or open an app by speaking to your device. Look for models with adjustable text sizes and high-contrast settings to make reading easier on your eyes. Tablets offer similar benefits but on a larger screen, which can be easier to navigate and read than smaller phone screens.

Setting up these devices might seem like a hurdle, but most are designed to be user-friendly right from the start. When you first switch on a new device, it typically launches a setup wizard. This step-by-step guide helps you connect to Wi-Fi, create user accounts, and adjust basic settings like language and accessibility options. Most devices also allow you to customize their operations to suit your needs, such as increasing font size or changing screen brightness. If you find yourself stuck during these initial steps, don't hesitate to ask a family member, a tech-savvy friend, or even staff at your local community center for help. Many communities offer free classes on using modern gadgets, which can be a great way to learn in a friendly, supportive environment.

Apps are the tools that truly unleash the potential of your smart devices. There are apps for nearly everything—managing medication schedules, ordering groceries delivered to your door, or arranging transportation. Apps like 'MyTherapy' remind you when to take your medicine, while 'Instacart' allows you to shop for groceries online from local stores and deliver them to your home. For transportation, ridesharing apps such as Uber or Lyft can provide a convenient alternative to driving, especially if you find driving at night or navigating heavy traffic less appealing than you used to.

Emergency Technology

One significant benefit of modern technology is how it enhances personal safety. Wearable emergency alert systems can be a lifeline in a crisis. Devices worn as pendants or wristbands are equipped with buttons to immediately call for help in an emergency, connecting you with emergency services or designated contacts. Additionally, apps that store your medical information and contact details can be invaluable in urgent situations, ensuring that first responders have immediate access to critical health data, which can sometimes mean the difference between life and death.

By embracing these technologies, you enhance your independence and connectivity, improving your ability to live safely and comfortably. While the tech world can sometimes seem overwhelming, taking it one step at a time, starting with mastering your devices' essential functions, can significantly enhance your quality of life. Remember, technology aims to make life easier and more enjoyable. With some patience and practice, you'll soon be navigating your devices like a pro, wondering how you ever managed without them.

Navigating Social Media Platforms Safely

Stepping into the world of social media can be like opening a window to a bustling, vibrant marketplace. Chatter, interaction, and a wealth of shared content unite communities from all corners of the globe. For us seniors, platforms like Facebook, Instagram, and X (formerly named Twitter) offer excellent opportunities to reconnect with old friends, keep up with family, and share the joys of our daily lives. Each platform has its flavor and style suited to different types of interactions. Facebook, for instance, is fantastic for joining groups of like-minded individuals, sharing updates, and participating in community discussions. With its focus on visual content, Instagram is ideal if you love photography or want to follow the visual stories of your family and friends. With its quick, real-time updates, Twitter can be great for staying informed about current events or following public figures.

However, with the benefits of these platforms comes the need for vigilance, especially about privacy and security. Navigating these settings starts with a basic understanding of each platform's privacy options. On Facebook, for instance, you can customize who sees your posts—whether it's just your friends, friends of friends, or the public. You can also control who can send you friend requests and who can look you up using your email address or phone number. Instagram and Twitter have similar settings, where you can make your account private, meaning only those you approve can see your posts. Taking control of these settings is the first step in securing your personal information and ensuring your online interactions remain within a circle you feel comfortable with.

Engaging on social media also comes with understanding what's appropriate to share and what's best kept private. It's wise to avoid posting sensitive personal information such as your home address, phone number, or financial details, which could be used maliciously. Additionally, think twice before sharing details about your daily routines or upcoming vacations, as this information could compromise your home security. Maintaining respect and kindness goes a long way when interacting with others, whether they are close friends or new online acquaintances. Social media should be a space for positive connection, not conflict or negativity. If you disagree, it's often best to take a step back and reflect rather than respond in the heat of the moment.

At times, you may encounter negative or inappropriate interactions online. If someone's behavior on these platforms makes you uncomfortable, most social media sites allow you to block or report the user. This action typically prevents them from seeing your posts or contacting you, and it flags their behavior for review by the platform's moderation team. If you're unsure how to use these features, ask someone you trust for help or look for online tutorials to guide you. Remember, it's important to prioritize your comfort and safety above all else.

Navigating social media safely and responsibly ensures your experience is enjoyable and enriching. By understanding the specific features of each platform, taking control of your privacy settings, engaging thoughtfully, and knowing how to handle negative interactions, you can make the most of these powerful tools for connection. These practices protect you and contribute to the positive and supportive atmosphere that makes social media such a fantastic place to connect and share. As you continue to explore and interact in these digital communities, you'll find they can offer wonderful ways to stay engaged and connected to the world around you, enriching your retirement life in countless ways.

Online Learning Platforms for Seniors

Retirement can also be a wonderful age of rediscovery and personal development, where learning new skills or deepening your knowledge on subjects of interest isn't just possible. It's also incredibly enriching. Thanks to the internet, the classroom is as close as your computer or tablet, opening up a world where physical locations or set schedules do not bind learning. Online platforms have revolutionized how we learn, offering flexibility that allows you to study at your own pace, at times that suit you, and in areas that truly capture your curiosity.

One of the most compelling advantages of online learning is its flexibility. Whether early bird or night owl, you can tailor your study schedule to fit your natural rhythm. This personalized approach can lead to more effective learning and greater enjoyment, which, let's face it, is what learning at this stage of life is all about—enjoyment and enrichment. Moreover, the breadth of subjects available online is staggering. Platforms like Coursera, Udemy, and Khan Academy offer courses ranging from the arts and music to science and technology taught by instructors from prestigious institutions and organizations worldwide. Whether you want to finally understand the intricacies of digital photography, explore historical events, or even dive into the basics of coding, these platforms have you covered.

Signing up for these courses is generally straightforward. Begin by visiting the website of the platform that interests you. You'll be prompted to create an account, usually requiring an email address and a password. From there, you can browse the course offerings. Many platforms allow you to filter courses by subject, difficulty level, and even by instructors. This can help you quickly find the courses that best match your interests and learning goals. Many courses are free, or for a small fee, you can gain additional access to more comprehensive course materials or earn a certificate of completion.

The interactive elements of online learning platforms are designed to enhance your educational experience and ensure deeper understanding and retention of the material. Discussion boards allow you to interact with fellow students from around the globe, offering new insights and perspectives that can enrich your learning experience. Quizzes and assignments help reinforce the material, providing practical experience and feedback. Video lectures, another key feature, allow you to see and hear experts discuss the topics you're learning about, which can be particularly helpful if you're exploring a new subject area.

Setting Realistic Learning Goals

To make the most of your online learning experience, it's important to set realistic and clear goals. Start by identifying why you want to take a particular course. Are you looking to develop a skill or explore out of pure interest? Perhaps you're considering turning a hobby into something more productive, or maybe you're seeking to keep your mind sharp by challenging it with new topics. Once your motivations are clear, set specific achievable and measurable goals. For instance, if you're taking a photography course, a goal might be to complete all modules and practice your skills by submitting a portfolio of photos as the final project. Keeping your goals achievable and aligned with your interests will help maintain your motivation and enjoyment throughout the learning process.

As you engage with these online platforms, remember that the learning journey is personal and should be enjoyable. The pressure to perform is off, leaving you free to explore, make mistakes, and discover, all from the comfort of your home. This freedom enhances the joy of learning and encourages you to take risks and venture into areas you might not have considered before.

In wrapping up this exploration of online learning platforms for seniors, it's clear that these resources offer a fantastic opportunity to continue growing and learning in retirement. They provide flexible, diverse, and accessible educational options that can significantly enrich your life, allowing you to follow your interests at your own pace and on your terms. As we continue to explore technology's role in enhancing retirement, let's carry forward this spirit of openness and curiosity, embracing the tools that allow us to connect and learn in ways that were unimaginable just a few decades ago.

EIGHT

Exploring New Passions

Imagine a world where every moment, every detail of life can be captured and preserved forever—not just in memory, but in vivid, living color. Photography, a hobby that marries art with technology, offers a chance to freeze time and hold on to the now forever. Whether it's the grandeur of a sunset or the simple smile of a grandchild, photography allows you to keep these moments close, to revisit and relive them whenever you wish. It's a pursuit that can bring immense joy and satisfaction, especially in a phase of life where savoring every beautiful detail becomes even more meaningful.

Photography as a Hobby: Capturing Life's Moments

Introduction to Photography

Diving into photography starts with choosing your tool—your camera. Today's market offers an array of cameras suited for beginners, from point-and-shoot models to more advanced DSLRs and mirrorless cameras. Each type has its benefits: point-and-shoot cameras, for instance, are compact and user-friendly, perfect for those who prefer something straightforward and convenient. With their interchangeable lenses and manual settings, DSLRs offer greater flexibility and control, which is ideal for capturing higher-quality images that reflect your vision.

Choosing the right camera often depends on what you want to achieve. Are you looking to document family events and gatherings with clear, vibrant photos? A high-quality point-and-shoot might be perfect. Or perhaps you're interested in exploring the nuances of light and shadow or the delicate details of nature—then a DSLR might be your best companion. Visiting a camera store and talking to knowledgeable staff can help you make an informed decision. They can guide you through the different models, letting you handle them to feel what suits your hands and style best.

Learning the Art

Mastering photography is a journey—a delightful and rewarding one. Numerous resources are available to help you along the way. Online courses offer convenience and breadth, covering everything from basic photography skills to advanced techniques. Websites like Udemy or Coursera host courses taught by seasoned photographers, providing invaluable insights and tips for beginners and more experienced enthusiasts.

Local workshops are another fantastic resource. They offer hands-on learning experiences that can be deeply enriching.

These workshops teach you technical skills and allow you to connect with fellow photography enthusiasts in your community. This can add a social element to your learning, making it even more enjoyable.

Books on photography can also be a great addition to your learning toolkit. They provide comprehensive guides on techniques, composition, and even the history of photography, allowing you to learn at your own pace and refer back to them as needed. Libraries and bookstores often have sections dedicated to photography books, ranging from beginner guides to advanced manuals.

Photography Projects to Start With

Starting with simple projects can help build your confidence and skills. A 'photo a day' challenge is a fantastic way to begin. It encourages you to take at least one photo daily, which can quickly improve your skills and help you see the world through a photographer's eye. You might choose a specific theme for a month—like nature, the people in your life, or the places you visit—or let your inspiration guide you.

Thematic photo collections can also be rewarding. Consider focusing on a theme such as "joy," capturing whatever reflects this emotion. People laughing, a peaceful landscape, or a scene from your daily life that brings you joy. These themes can guide your observations and help you develop a more thoughtful approach to what you capture.

Sharing and Preserving Photos

Once you have a collection of photos, sharing them can be both exciting and rewarding. Social media platforms like Instagram and Facebook are popular places to share images with friends and family. They allow you to post your photos, get feedback, and engage with others who share your interests. Creating a personal blog can also be a wonderful way to share your journey in photography, allowing you more space to tell the stories behind your photos and interact with a broader audience.

Preserving your photographs is just as important as taking them. Printing your favorite shots and creating photo albums or scrapbooks can be a delightful way to keep these memories alive. These physical copies are personal keepsakes and can be wonderful gifts for friends and family. They allow you to pass down memories and moments through generations, turning your hobby into a legacy of captured time.

With its power to capture and preserve the fleeting moments of our lives, photography offers a unique blend of artistic expression and personal fulfillment. Whether you're documenting the major events of your life or the quiet daily moments, each photo serves as a testament to the beauty and richness of your world. As you explore this art, you'll find that each picture adds depth to your days, turning the ordinary into something extraordinary, one snapshot at a time.

Gardening for Relaxation and Nutrition

Gardening, often seen merely as a hobby, holds a deeper, more gratifying essence, especially as we step into the later chapters of our lives. There's a certain magic in tending to a garden, a rhythmic, almost meditative quality that can soothe busy minds and provide a gentle yet effective form of exercise. Beyond its calming effects, gardening invites you to nurture life from the soil—watching as seeds you plant and tend grow into flourishing plants that can feed your body with their fresh produce and nourish your soul with a sense of accomplishment and connection to nature.

The therapeutic benefits of gardening are manifold. Engaging with the earth, whether turning the soil or planting seeds, offers a physical activity that's both gentle and invigorating, suitable for varying levels of mobility. This connection with the earth can significantly alleviate stress. As you focus on the needs of your plants, daily anxieties tend to slip away, replaced by a focus on the nurturing acts of watering, pruning, and caring for your plants. The satisfaction of seeing your garden thrive can also boost your mood and self-esteem, providing tangible rewards for your efforts.

Starting your garden is an adventure in creativity and patience, beginning with understanding your space and the environment. You might designate a corner for a small vegetable or herb garden if you have a backyard. For those with limited space, container gardening can be an excellent alternative. Containers can be placed on balconies, patios, or window sills. The key is to choose the right containers and soil mix to ensure proper growth.

Additionally, understanding your local climate is crucial. To ensure success, select plants suited to your area's weather conditions. Local gardening centers often provide regional planting guides, which can be invaluable in helping you choose plants that will thrive in your environment.

Maintaining a garden requires regular attention, but it's more manageable than it might seem. Establishing a routine for watering, weeding, and monitoring your plants for pests can make maintenance manageable and enjoyable. For instance, early morning or late afternoon watering can reduce evaporation and ensure that your plants get the moisture they need. Regular weeding keeps your garden tidy and ensures that your plants aren't competing for nutrients. As for pests, natural remedies such as neem oil or homemade insecticidal soaps can protect your garden without harsh chemicals.

Harvesting your produce is the most rewarding part of gardening. There's a profound joy in picking your labor's fruits (or vegetables), which can be transformed into nutritious and delicious meals. Fresh herbs can elevate the simplest dishes, while vegetables like tomatoes, peppers, and leafy greens can form the basis of many healthy recipes. For instance, a simple salad freshly picked from your garden can be more flavorful than any store-bought alternative. Moreover, preserving your harvest through techniques like freezing, drying, or canning can allow you to enjoy your garden's bounty year-round. Freezing is particularly effective for many vegetables and fruits, retaining their nutritional value and flavor. Drying herbs is another easy preservation method, ensuring you have a supply of aromatic flavors at your fingertips whenever you cook.

Engaging in gardening enhances your physical and mental well-being and connects you to an enriching and grounding cycle of life. As you sow, tend, and harvest, you're reminded of the rhythms of nature and your place within it. Each season brings its joys and challenges; through gardening, you experience the fullness of life's continuous unfolding.

The Joy of Painting in Retirement

Painting is like opening a window in your mind, allowing you to express your inner visions and emotions on a canvas. It's a wonderfully immersive activity that invites you to mix, blend, and bring your thoughts to life through colors and strokes. Painting in retirement can be especially rewarding, offering a creative outlet that is both soothing and stimulating. Whether you work with oils, watercolors, or acrylics, each medium has its unique charm and techniques, catering to different styles and preferences.

For those just starting, the variety of painting supplies and techniques might seem overwhelming, but the joy of painting lies in its accessibility. Acrylics are often recommended for beginners due to their versatility and relatively quick drying times. With their delicate and translucent qualities, watercolors are ideal for capturing landscapes and subtle color shifts. While more challenging, oils offer richer colors and greater depth, allowing for detailed and textured effects. Starting with simpler and more affordable materials can make the process more manageable. Many art stores offer starter kits that include basic palettes, brushes, and canvases, which are perfect for beginners. The key is experimenting with different materials and finding what feels right for you, remembering that each brushstroke improves your skill and confidence.

Finding inspiration for your paintings can be as simple as looking around you. The beauty of a garden, the tranquility of a quiet street, or the vibrancy of a bustling market can all translate into stunning artwork. Travel to local parks or foreign lands can also provide a diverse array of scenes and experiences to capture. Keeping a sketchbook handy allows you to jot down and sketch ideas as they come, serving as a personal repository of inspiration. This sketchbook can be your companion, where you practice sketches, play with color combinations, or write notes about the scenes and subjects that move you.

The social aspect of painting can be as enriching as the creative process itself. Many communities offer art classes tailored to various skill levels, providing a structured environment where you can learn new techniques and meet other art enthusiasts. These classes enhance your skills and build a community of like-minded individuals who share your passion for art. For those who prefer a more flexible schedule, online platforms like Skillshare or YouTube host countless tutorials and courses where you can learn at your own pace.

Beyond personal fulfillment, painting offers opportunities to share and even monetize your art. Displaying your paintings at home can transform your living space, turning walls into personal galleries that reflect your journey and style. Gifting artwork to loved ones creates meaningful presents that carry your personal touch and the stories behind each piece. Furthermore, local art fairs and online platforms like Etsy provide venues to sell your artwork. Participating in these fairs can be a delightful experience, allowing you to engage with the public and other artists, and seeing someone appreciate and purchase your art is incredibly validating.

In essence, painting in retirement opens up a world of creative possibilities. It allows you to express yourself, preserve memories, and connect with others through the universal language of art. As you explore this enriching activity, you'll discover that each brushstroke colors the canvas and enhances your life, adding vibrancy and joy to your retirement years.

As we conclude this chapter on exploring new passions through photography, gardening, and painting, we see a pattern of enrichment and growth that these activities bring to our lives. They provide hobbies and gateways to developing new skills, forming social connections, and expressing creativity. As we turn the page to the next chapter, we'll delve into the enriching world of travel, exploring how discovering new places and cultures can further enhance our retirement experience.

NINE

The Traveling Senior

Picture the gentle sway of palm trees against a serene sunset, the soft sand underfoot, and the soothing sound of waves—an idyllic backdrop for anyone, but especially poignant as a scene of relaxation in your retirement years. Travel in retirement isn't just about seeing new places; it's about experiencing the world through a lens of leisure and depth that only comes with the wisdom of your years. This chapter is your companion on this delightful venture, guiding you through making the most of every trip without straining your budget.

Planning Your Dream Vacation on a Budget

Traveling can be one of the most enriching experiences, but without careful planning, it can also become one of the most expensive. However, your years of experience have equipped you with the wisdom to appreciate that the most memorable moments don't always have to come with a hefty price tag. Let's explore how to stretch your travel dollars further, ensuring each journey is enjoyable and economically savvy.

Utilizing budget travel strategies starts with choosing when and how you travel. Traveling during off-peak seasons can save airfare, accommodations, and attractions. For instance, visiting Europe in the fall or late winter instead of summer can not only cut costs but also enhance your experience by avoiding the crowds. Airlines and hotels often offer lower rates during these times to encourage travel, so take advantage of these periods. Additionally, consider the benefits of budget airlines for shorter flights. While they may offer fewer amenities, the savings can be substantial, and let's be honest, the joy of travel is found in the destination, not just the journey.

Choosing cost-effective accommodations like Airbnb or senior hostels can also reduce expenses. These options offer a more local experience and often provide access to a kitchen, allowing you to save money by preparing some of your meals. Many of these accommodations also offer the charm of personal touches that can make your stay more memorable than a standard hotel room.

Leveraging senior discounts is another crucial strategy. Did you know many travel agencies, airlines, and rail services offer discounts for seniors? These can range from reduced airfares to cheaper rail passes. Always inquire about senior rates when booking your travel; sometimes, they are not prominently advertised but can provide significant savings. For example, many European rail passes offer senior discounts, making travel scenic and affordable.

Planning and budgeting wisely for your trip is the most crucial step. List all potential expenses: transportation, accommodations, meals, entertainment, and travel insurance. Tools like budget calculators, available on many travel websites, can help you estimate your total costs and keep track of your spending. Websites and apps designed for senior travel can be beneficial. They often feature user reviews from fellow senior travelers, which can provide insights into how suitable specific accommodations, activities, or tours might be for your needs and preferences. Resources like the Senior Travel Expert or the AARP Travel Center offer tailored advice and discounts, making them invaluable tools in your travel planning arsenal.

Interactive Element: Travel Budget Worksheet

Consider using a travel budget worksheet to plan your expenses. List your estimated costs for each trip category, track your expenses, and adjust your budget as needed. This simple tool can help you manage your finances smoothly, ensuring you stay within your budget without compromising on the experiences you wish to enjoy.

By adopting these thoughtful travel strategies—from choosing the right time to pick budget-friendly accommodations to leveraging senior discounts and meticulously planning your budget—you can ensure that each trip is as enriching as it is economical. Travel in retirement is not just about ticking destinations off your list; it's about making memories that enrich your life without draining your finances.

Must-Visit Destinations for Cultural Enrichment

Imagine strolling through the cobbled streets of Rome, where every corner boasts centuries-old architecture and every museum houses masterpieces by legends like Michelangelo and

Caravaggio. Or envision yourself at the vibrant festivals of India, surrounded by a kaleidoscope of colors and the rhythmic beats of traditional music. Maybe you're walking the ancient paths of Machu Picchu in Peru, breathing in the history that whispers through the ruins. These experiences are travels and cultural immersions that enrich the soul and broaden the mind.

Exploring culturally rich destinations offers more than just sightseeing. It's about engaging deeply with the history, art, and traditions that have shaped civilizations. Italy, for example, is not just a hub for art and architecture but a tape yard for understanding the Renaissance, the pivotal era that reshaped Europe. The cities of Florence, Venice, and Rome are living museums, offering endless opportunities to encounter works that have transcended time. With its diverse cultures and deep spiritual heritage, India provides an entirely different palette of experiences. From the Taj Mahal's architectural splendor to Varanasi's spiritual serenity, India's diverse history and spirituality offer profound insights into human creativity and religious devotion. Peru, known for its archaeological sites, showcases the ingenuity of ancient civilizations and offers a stunning display of how nature and human endeavor can coexist beautifully.

For seniors, engaging with these cultures can be made comfortable and accessible through senior-friendly cultural tours. These tours are thoughtfully designed to accommodate the needs of older travelers, offering slower-paced itineraries and more comfortable accommodations. They often include expert guides who provide rich narratives that enhance the historical and cultural understanding of the sites visited. When selecting a cultural tour, it's important to consider the itinerary's physical demands, pace, and the level of comfort provided. Many travel companies now offer reviews and ratings to help you choose a tour that fits your physical capabilities and travel desires. Companies like Road Scholar and ElderTreks specialize in educational and adventure travel tailored to older adults who wish to explore the world in comfort and depth.

Immersing yourself in local cultures extends beyond sightseeing; it involves engaging with the people and their traditions. Learning a few phrases in the local language enriches your interaction and shows respect for the culture. Simple greetings, expressions of thanks, and common courtesies can open doors to more engaging conversations and deeper understanding. Participating in local cooking classes or craft workshops allows you to delve into the locals' everyday lives, learn skills passed down through generations, and experience the culture hands-on. These activities provide a unique learning experience and create opportunities to connect with others with similar interests.

Documenting and sharing your journey can enhance the experience and allow you to relive the memories long after the trip has ended. Keeping a travel journal or blog serves as a personal record of your adventures and discoveries. You can jot down details about the places you visit, the people you meet, and the emotions you experience. Photos and sketches add a visual dimension to your stories, capturing moments that words alone might not fully encompass. Sharing these experiences through a blog or social media keeps you connected with family and friends. It inspires others to explore and appreciate our world's vast cultural richness. Tools like online blogs or platforms such as Instagram or Facebook can make sharing easy and interactive, allowing you to keep a digital diary that friends and family can visit, comment on, and enjoy.

Exploring new cultures and destinations in retirement isn't just about adding stamps to your passport; it's about enriching your life with experiences that educate, inspire, and delight. Whether through the art-laden streets of Italy, the colorful festivals of India, or the historic paths of Peru, each journey offers unique experiences that deepen your understanding of the world and your appreciation for its diverse cultures.

Travel Tips for Physical Well-Being

Staying healthy while exploring new destinations is as crucial as the itinerary, ensuring every adventure is enjoyed thoroughly. Think of your health as your travel companion, needing attention and care to keep the journey smooth and delightful. Here are some thoughtful ways to maintain your well-being as you embrace the joys of travel.

Hydration is the cornerstone of health, more so while traveling. Changes in climates and activities can quickly lead to dehydration, catching you off guard during the excitement of exploring. Always carry a reusable water bottle, and remember to sip regularly throughout the day. Air travel, in particular, can dehydrate, so it's wise to increase your fluid intake before, during, and after your flight. If you're visiting a destination where the tap water isn't safe to drink, ensure you have access to bottled water or use a portable water purifier.

Managing medication across different time zones can be challenging but manageable with some planning. Use a pill organizer to keep your medication schedule consistent, and set reminders on your phone or watch. Calculating the time differences in advance is essential, and adjusting your medication schedule accordingly to maintain its effectiveness.

Consulting with your healthcare provider before your trip can provide additional guidance tailored to your health needs.

Proper rest and nutrition are pivotal in keeping you energized and healthy during your travels. It's tempting to push your limits to soak in as much as possible but remember, adequate rest is key to enjoying your experiences fully. Try to maintain a regular sleep schedule, and allow yourself short naps to recover from a long day of adventures. Nutrition-wise, try to balance indulging in local cuisines with maintaining a diet that supports your energy levels and health. Include plenty of fruits, vegetables, and proteins to keep your body well-fueled for the journey.

Travel insurance is essential for planning for the unforeseen. Ensure your policy covers pre-existing conditions and includes health coverage for medical treatments abroad. Check whether your insurance offers direct payments to hospitals or if you'll need to pay upfront and seek reimbursement. Knowing these details can alleviate stress if you need medical assistance during your trip, letting you focus on your recovery rather than paperwork.

Packing Essentials for Health and Safety

Before you set off, packing a well-thought-out health kit can make a significant difference. Essential items should include your medications, copies of your prescriptions, and a basic first aid kit equipped with bandages, antiseptic wipes, and some common over-the-counter medicines for aches, allergies, or indigestion. Don't forget to pack comfortable footwear, especially if your trip involves a lot of walking. Good shoes can prevent foot and joint pain, making your travel experience more enjoyable. Sunscreen and hats are also important, protecting you from harmful UV rays on a sunny beach or strolling through a bustling city.

Finding medical assistance abroad might feel daunting, but a little preparation can ease this concern. Research the medical facilities near your destinations before you leave, especially if you have ongoing health conditions. Most embassies and consulates can provide information on nearby clinics and hospitals that offer services in English. Additionally, carrying a list of emergency contacts, including your family members, your hotel, and your country's embassy, along with a medical information card that lists your health conditions, medications, and allergies, ensures you can receive appropriate care quickly if needed.

By paying attention to these health and safety aspects, your travels can be memorable, comfortable and worry-free. Ensuring you are well-prepared allows you to immerse yourself fully in the splendors of new environments and cultures without health worries casting a shadow over your experiences.

As we close this chapter on travel, remember that every trip is an opportunity to enrich your life with new sights, sounds, and stories. Taking care of your health ensures that each journey is as joyful as enriching, weaving together the experiences that celebrate the freedom and adventure that retirement affords. Next, we'll explore how to adjust your living space to reflect this vibrant phase of life, ensuring your home is as comfortable and welcoming as the many destinations you've enjoyed.

TEN

Home Sweet Home: Adapting Your Living Space

Imagine waking up each morning in a home that feels just right—where every nook is familiar, every cranny optimized for comfort, and every space echoes your life's chapters with warmth and functionality. As we move through different stages of life, our living spaces can also evolve to reflect and accommodate our changing needs and desires. For many, a significant part of this evolution in retirement might involve the decision to downsize. This isn't just about moving to a smaller space—it's about reshaping your environment to enhance your lifestyle, making daily life easier and more enjoyable.

Downsizing: Making the Big Move Smoother

The thought of downsizing can evoke emotions—from the excitement of starting a fresh chapter to the nostalgia and apprehension about leaving a familiar place filled with memories. Let's navigate this transition together, ensuring that the decision to downsize and the following process is as smooth and positive as possible.

Assessing the Need to Downsize

First, consider why downsizing might be right for you at this moment. Is it the financial benefits of a smaller home with lower maintenance costs and utility bills? Perhaps the physical aspect—fewer rooms to clean and less yard to manage can significantly reduce the daily strain, making your living situation more comfortable as mobility becomes a concern. Or maybe it's for social reasons—moving to a community of peers where social activities and amenities are just a short walk away. Evaluating your living situation against these factors can help clarify whether downsizing is practical. Reflect on what aspects of your current home might limit your lifestyle or add unnecessary stress. Is the garden that once brought joy now just a list of chores? Are the empty rooms serving any purpose other than collecting dust? These reflections can help you decide what aligns with your current needs and future happiness.

Choosing the Right New Home

Once you decide downsizing is the right step, selecting your new home is the next crucial phase. This choice should be about convenience and accessibility. Look for a home that simplifies life: single-level layouts can be a boon, eliminating the need to navigate stairs daily. Consider the location relative to critical amenities—how close is the nearest hospital, the pharmacy, the grocery store, or public transport? Proximity to these services can significantly impact your quality of life, especially if driving long distances is something you prefer to avoid. Also, think about the social opportunities a new place offers. Are there community centers, parks, or clubs nearby?

Are social activities and gatherings a part of the community schedule? These elements can greatly enhance your social life and ensure you remain active and engaged.

Efficiently Sorting and Decluttering

Sorting through a lifetime of possessions can be the most daunting part of downsizing. Here's a systematic approach: start by categorizing items into what to keep, sell, donate, or discard. Focus on keeping things that are necessary or hold significant sentimental value. Be realistic about what fits in your new space and lifestyle. For items with emotional attachments that are too large or impractical to take with you, consider taking photos of them before letting go. This way, you keep the memories, even if you no longer have the physical items. Organize a yard sale or use online platforms to sell items in good condition that won't fit in your new home. Donating items can also provide a sense of fulfillment, knowing that your belongings will help someone in need. Managing the emotional aspect of this process is crucial; acknowledge that it's okay to feel sentimental or reluctant to let go. It might help to have family or friends who can offer emotional support and assist with the practicalities of sorting and packing.

Streamlining the Moving Process

When the time comes to move, organization is key. Hiring reliable movers who specialize in helping seniors can make the process smoother. Ensure that these movers are reputable and sensitive to the needs of older adults. Plan the moving day with precision: label boxes clearly, ensure essentials are easily accessible, and, if possible, set up key areas like the bedroom and bathroom first in your new home. This organization minimizes stress and confusion, allowing you to settle in quickly and comfortably.

By carefully assessing the need to downsize, choosing the right new home, efficiently sorting through belongings, and streamlining the moving process, you can ensure that downsizing enhances your life. It will offer you a living space that is not only more manageable but also opens new opportunities for enjoyment and fulfillment in your retirement years. As you settle into your new home, you may find it not just a place of residence but a new beginning filled with potential and promise, tailor-made for the next chapter of your life.

Safety Modifications for the Aging at Home

As the places we live evolve with us, ensuring they remain safe and supportive of our needs becomes a priority that can't be overlooked. It's much like tending to a beloved garden; it requires care, attention, and sometimes, restructuring to ensure it thrives. For many of us in our later years, our homes must be more than just comfortable—they must be safe and easy to navigate. This can mean making several modifications, from simple additions to more significant changes, each aimed at reducing risks and enhancing our ability to move freely and safely around our space.

Let's talk about some essential safety upgrades first. Installing bathroom grab bars is a practical step to make a significant difference. These sturdy supports can help prevent falls, one of the seniors' most common accidents at home, especially in slippery areas like showers and tubs. Similarly, improving lighting in hallways, staircases, and other common areas is crucial. Adequate lighting not only helps in avoiding obstacles but also in maintaining balance and coordination, which can sometimes falter as we age. Another simple yet effective modification is removing trip hazards throughout the home, such as loose carpets, cluttered walkways, and uneven flooring. These changes might seem minor, but they can dramatically reduce the likelihood of falls and accidents, ensuring your home remains a haven.

Moving on to technology, several innovative solutions can further enhance the safety of your home. Medical alert systems, for example, are devices designed to call for help at the push of a button. Worn as a pendant or bracelet, these devices can be lifesavers in emergencies, providing peace of mind for you and your family. Motion sensor lights are another fantastic addition, illuminating spaces when movement is detected. This is particularly useful for night-time navigation, automatically providing light through dark corridors or rooms. Smart home devices can also play a pivotal role in home safety. Features like automatic stove turn-off systems and water leak detectors can help prevent common household accidents. At the same time, smart locks can enhance home security, allowing you to lock and unlock doors remotely without needing to reach for high or awkwardly placed locks physically.

Regular maintenance checks are the backbone of a safe and functional home. Just as you regularly check a car to ensure it's running smoothly, your home requires the same attention to detail. Smoke detectors, carbon monoxide detectors, and fire extinguishers should be checked regularly to ensure they are in working order. Servicing major appliances can prevent malfunctions that might lead to accidents or emergencies. Similarly, maintaining your heating and cooling systems ensures that your home remains comfortable and prevents issues like overheating or excessive cooling, which can be hazardous, especially for seniors.

Lastly, designing for accessibility can significantly enhance the comfort and usability of your home. Simple changes like replacing traditional door knobs with lever handles can make a big difference for those with limited hand strength or dexterity. Installing ramps or stairlifts can provide easy access to homes with steps or levels while remodeling kitchens and bathrooms to be more ergonomic and wheelchair-friendly can transform these spaces into safe, easy-to-navigate areas. These modifications improve safety and foster independence, allowing you to enjoy your home confidently and easily.

By integrating these safety upgrades, embracing helpful technology, conducting regular maintenance, and designing with accessibility in mind, your home can continue to be a source of comfort and joy, adapting to your needs and ensuring your well-being in every corner.

Eco-Friendly Home Adjustments for Sustainable Living

There's something truly fulfilling about turning your home into a green sanctuary, where every adjustment contributes to your comfort and savings and plays a part in safeguarding the planet for future generations. Embracing eco-friendly home adjustments can be a rewarding journey, enhancing your living space while aligning with your values of sustainability and responsibility. Let's explore how small changes in your home can significantly benefit the environment, your health, and your wallet.

The environmental benefits of an eco-friendly home are well-documented. Still, they're worth reiterating because they directly impact the world, your immediate surroundings, and your quality of life. By reducing your home's energy consumption through various green adjustments, you're contributing less to greenhouse gas emissions and pollution, major factors in global warming and environmental degradation. Health benefits are equally compelling; eco-friendly homes often use materials and technologies that improve air and water quality, reducing the risk of illnesses associated with pollutants and contaminants commonly found in less green households. Financially, while some green upgrades require upfront investment, the return is tangible—lower utility bills, reduced maintenance costs, and even potential tax incentives can make these adjustments financially advantageous in the long run.

Let's dive into the specifics, starting with energy-efficient appliances and fixtures. When it's time to replace old appliances, opting for those that are Energy Star certified can significantly affect your home's energy consumption. Energy Star appliances, including refrigerators, washers, and dryers, are designed to use minimal electricity and water, which not only helps the environment but also lowers your utility bills. Similarly, water-saving fixtures such as low-flow toilets and showerheads reduce water usage dramatically. A low-flow showerhead, for example, can save up to 2,700 gallons of water per year. Installing these fixtures is usually straightforward and can often be done without professional help, making them an easy yet effective upgrade.

Improving home insulation is another key area to enhance your home's energy efficiency. Proper insulation helps maintain your home's temperature, reducing the need for winter heating and summer cooling. Consider adding additional insulation to your attic and walls and replacing old windows with energy-efficient ones to prevent heat loss. Sealing leaks around doors and windows with weather stripping or caulk can also prevent drafts and improve your home's insulation. These adjustments make your home more comfortable and reduce the energy needed to heat or cool it, decreasing your carbon footprint and energy bills.

Lastly, adopting renewable energy solutions is one of the most impactful steps to creating a sustainable home. Solar panels are the most common option, allowing you to generate clean electricity. While the initial setup cost can be significant, the long-term savings are substantial, and many governments offer incentives, rebates, or tax breaks to offset the installation costs. Additionally, participating in green energy programs offered by local utilities can allow you to support renewable energy production even if installing solar panels isn't feasible for your situation. These programs often involve a small premium on your energy bill but can be a worthwhile investment in supporting environmental sustainability.

Making your home eco-friendly is a step towards a sustainable lifestyle that respects the planet and provides a healthier, more cost-effective living environment. These adjustments, from installing energy-efficient appliances to adopting renewable energy solutions, contribute to a greener earth and enhance your everyday life by creating a comfortable and cost-effective home. As you continue to make these positive changes, you're not just upgrading your home but investing in a better future for yourself and future generations.

In wrapping up this chapter, we've explored how making thoughtful, sustainable choices in your home can lead to a healthier environment, improved personal well-being, and substantial financial savings. Each step towards an eco-friendly home is towards a more sustainable and fulfilling lifestyle. The next chapter will look forward to the joys and challenges of intergenerational living, opening up new ways to enrich your family life and deepen your connections across generations.

ELEVEN

Intergenerational Bonding

Imagine a warm Sunday afternoon, the air filled with the laughter of your family as you gather around a backyard table adorned with your latest project—a collection of family recipes passed down through generations, now bound into a beautiful homemade cookbook. This scene isn't just a delightful gathering but a bridge connecting different generations through shared heritage and creativity. In retirement, you have a unique opportunity to be the architect of such bridges, crafting experiences that bring your family together and pass on valuable traditions, skills, and stories. This chapter explores how you can make the most of these opportunities, enriching your family and your own.

Family Projects That Bridge the Generational Gap

Family projects are a wonderful way to gather different generations around a common goal or interest. These activities should be accessible and enjoyable for all ages, ensuring that everyone, from the youngest grandchild to the eldest family member, can participate meaningfully. Let's delve into how you can select and adapt projects to include everyone, making these moments educational and enjoyable.

Choosing inclusive activities is key. For instance, family history research can captivate members of all ages. You might start with storytelling sessions where older relatives share their memories and experiences. These stories can then be the basis for a family tree project, with younger members researching additional details online or through library archives. Gardening is another inclusive activity. Setting up a family garden allows members to contribute differently. The younger ones could handle the planting under your guidance while you manage more strenuous tasks like pruning. Cooking traditional family recipes is also a fantastic way to bond. Organize a cooking day where each generation teaches the others a favorite recipe. This preserves the culinary heritage and creates a delicious experience shared by all.

The benefits of shared creative projects are immense. Engaging in activities like crafting, painting, or building model kits together isn't just about the tangible outcomes, although these can be quite rewarding. More importantly, these activities foster communication, teach teamwork, and often require problem-solving. They allow each family member to contribute unique skills and perspectives, enhancing generational appreciation and understanding. For example, while building a model airplane, the older generation can share stories about their experiences with aviation. At the same time, younger members might contribute by finding historical facts online or teaching older members how to use new crafting tools or techniques.

Organizing Family Events

Organizing recurring family events such as game nights, movie nights, or seasonal crafts offers a structured opportunity for regular gatherings that can become cherished family traditions. Consider a monthly game night where games are chosen to suit all ages or a movie night where films from different eras are enjoyed, sparking conversations about changes in culture and technology. Seasonal crafts, like making holiday decorations, involve everyone in creating a festive environment and making memories revisited year after year.

These gatherings are fun and a canvas for teaching and learning across generations. Use these projects as opportunities to pass on valuable skills. If you're adept at woodworking, organize a simple workshop for the family to make birdhouses. This teaches them a skill about local wildlife and the importance of conservation. Sewing or knitting gatherings can result in lovely handmade gifts while teaching patience and precision. Financial literacy projects, such as planning a family budget or understanding investments, can be invaluable, especially for younger members.

Intergenerational bonding through shared projects and organized events strengthens family ties and enhances social and emotional well-being. It turns the wealth of your experience into a legacy of shared memories and learned skills, enriching your family's story with knowledge, creativity, and affection. As you continue these activities, remember each moment spent together builds a bridge to a united, supportive family dynamic that spans the breadth of generations, enriching every family member with a more profound sense of connection and belonging.

Using Technology to Connect with Grandchildren

In this age where digital fluency is a given for the younger generation, embracing technology can transform how you connect with your grandchildren, making distances shrink and allowing shared experiences despite physical separation. Think of technology as a bridge; on one side, you have your rich reservoir of experiences and stories, and on the other, your grandchildren with their quick, tech-savvy minds. Bridging this gap can bring you closer, creating a shared space where both generations teach and learn from each other.

Introducing technology as a bonding tool is like opening a treasure chest filled with endless possibilities. Have you considered playing video games with your grandchildren? While it might sound daunting, video games can be a vibrant avenue for connection. Games like 'Minecraft' allow players to build worlds together, offering a fantastic way to collaborate and communicate creatively while having fun. Alternatively, apps that support stargazing and learning about constellations can turn a simple night under the stars into an educational adventure that sparks wonder and curiosity. For a more immersive experience, virtual reality (VR) can be exhilarating. Imagine traveling through the human bloodstream in a VR science app or exploring ancient civilizations in a history-themed VR experience. These activities are not just entertaining; they're gateways to discovery and discussion, making learning a dynamic, interactive experience that bridges generations.

Turning to educational tech tools, many apps and online platforms cater to learning in engaging and interactive ways. Language learning apps like Duolingo offer a playful approach to mastering a new language together, allowing you and your grandchildren to challenge each other in friendly competitions or celebrate milestones. For those fascinated by the wonders of science, websites like NASA's Kids' Club provide interactive games and tutorials that make understanding the universe fun and accessible. Engaging in these learning experiences together can be incredibly rewarding, giving you a glimpse into your grandchildren's world and allowing them to see you as a lifelong learner.

Social media also offers a robust platform for staying connected with your grandchildren. It can be a window into their lives, allowing you to witness their achievements, interests, and daily adventures. However, navigating social media requires a gentle touch. Respecting their space online is important, just as you would in person. Engage with their posts positively and thoughtfully—commenting on their achievements, sharing posts that remind you of good times spent together, or posting pictures of family gatherings. But it's also crucial to maintain a balance, ensuring your interactions are supportive without overwhelming. This respectful engagement helps strengthen your relationship, showing them that you are interested and involved in their world, even from afar.

Lastly, establishing regular tech-based communication routines can significantly enhance your connection. Scheduled video calls can become anticipated, especially if they coincide with special occasions like birthdays or holidays. Sharing photos regularly through family-shared albums or apps keeps the family feeling close, even if they are miles apart. Consider starting a family blog where each member contributes posts about their lives, thoughts, or experiences. This can be an excellent way to keep up with each other's lives in a more detailed and personal way than social media allows.

Using digital tools in family life can help you stay connected and better understand each other. When used thoughtfully, technology isn't just a tool for communication; it becomes a conduit for sharing, learning, and loving, bringing different generations together in a world increasingly driven by digital interaction. Embracing this can make your golden years even more golden, filled with the laughter and closeness of family, regardless of the miles between you.

Sharing Life Lessons and Legacy Building

Each person's stories and wisdom are significant and unique. As you step into the later chapters of your story, you hold a wealth of experiences and insights that can serve as invaluable guideposts for future generations. Imagine compiling these into a legacy document or book—a tangible expression of your life's journey that can enlighten and inspire your children, grandchildren, and even those who will come long after you.

Creating a legacy document is like planting a tree under whose shade you may never sit but will provide comfort and shelter for others in the future. Start by reflecting on the milestones, the challenges overcome, and the joys experienced throughout your life. These can form the chapters of your book or the themes of your series of letters. Consider the format that best suits your style—some might prefer writing detailed memoirs in a digital format that can easily be shared and preserved. In contrast, others might feel drawn to the intimacy of handwritten letters, which carry the personal touch of their script. Tools like online blogs or print-on-demand services can help you assemble and publish your memories in a professional yet personal way.

Storytelling is an art, and its power lies in its ability to connect and teach without seeming to do so. When sharing your life lessons with younger family members, focus on stories that resonate with universal themes such as love, resilience, and integrity. Craft these stories to be engaging, peppering them with vivid details, the emotions you felt, and the lessons you learned. For instance, recount the story of a significant setback, focusing not just on the event but on how you dealt with it, what it taught you about patience, or how it changed your perspective. These stories can be shared during family gatherings, or you could record them as audio files or videos, which can be particularly captivating for the younger, visually-oriented generation.

Involving your grandchildren in documenting your personal history is not just about preserving the past—it's about building connections. Encourage them to interview you, a process through which they can learn about their heritage and see the historical and personal events that have shaped their world. Together, you could create a family tree that goes beyond names and dates, adding stories, photographs, and notable attributes of family members. Visiting places of historical significance to your family can turn an abstract past into a tangible experience, making the family's history a vivid part of the grandchildren's reality.

Creating an ethical will is another profound way to share your values and wisdom. This is not a legal document but a heartfelt expression of what truly matters to you. Unlike a traditional will, which outlines how you wish to distribute your assets, an ethical will is about passing down ethical values, blessings, personal philosophies, and hopes for the future. It's a chance to articulate what you stand for and to voice your aspirations for your loved ones. Crafting such a document can be a reflective and clarifying experience, helping you distill the essence of what you've learned about living a meaningful life.

Through these activities—creating a legacy document, teaching through storytelling, involving your family in personal history projects, and sharing your values through an ethical will—you do more than preserve your legacy. You foster a deeper understanding and bond with your family, bridging generational divides with the threads of shared history and values. This endeavor not only enriches the lives of your descendants but also provides you with the satisfaction of knowing that your experiences will continue to inspire and guide you long after you are gone.

Reflecting on Our Shared Stories

As we wrap up this chapter on sharing life lessons and building your legacy, we touch upon something essential to human nature—the desire to be remembered, to leave something behind that outlasts our fleeting journey. The activities discussed here provide a way to fulfill this desire, letting you connect your past with your family's future. They enable you to contribute to a narrative that will continue to inspire, guide, and give comfort to those who come after you.

In the next chapter, we will explore creative expressions and intellectual pursuits that can enrich your retirement life and offer new avenues for personal growth and fulfillment. This continuation is about looking back and reaching forward into new experiences, learning, and self-discovery.

TWELVE

Creative Expression and Intellectual Pursuits

I magine it's a quiet morning where the sun casts a gentle glow through your window, inviting you to sit down with a cup of tea and reflect on the years that have painted the canvas of your life. This moment of reflection isn't just about nostalgia; it's about gathering your experiences and creating a narrative that can be shared and cherished. The art of writing memoirs, a profound journey into your past, offers a therapeutic release and an invaluable legacy for those who come after you. This chapter will explore how you can capture the essence of your life's stories, preserving your memories and lessons in the timeless form of written words.

Writing Your Memoirs

Understanding the Value of Memoirs

Writing your memoirs is more than just documenting events; it's about capturing the emotions, the lessons, and the transitions that have defined your journey. Each chapter of your life, from childhood adventures to career challenges and family milestones, holds unique insights and wisdom that can benefit future generations. Memoirs allow you to reflect on and understand your experiences more deeply, offering emotional catharsis and a profound sense of closure or acceptance. They serve as a bridge between generations, a way for your grandchildren and their children to know who you were beyond photographs and family stories and to learn from the life you've lived.

Guidance on Structuring Your Memoirs

Crafting a memoir requires thoughtful structure to capture and communicate your life story effectively. Start by outlining the key moments that you believe define your journey. These could be pivotal decisions, significant events, or moments of personal evolution. Organize these events chronologically or group them around central themes such as resilience, love, learning, or growth. Each chapter of your memoir could focus on a specific phase of your life or a particular theme, weaving together narratives that provide a cohesive insight into your experiences.

Creating a compelling narrative involves more than just laying out the facts; it requires you to delve into the emotions and implications of your experiences. Reflect on how each event shaped you: What did you learn? How did you change? This reflective approach enriches your memoir and enhances its impact on readers, allowing them to draw parallels to their lives and lessons.

Techniques for Effective Writing

To truly bring your memoirs to life, employ writing techniques that enhance storytelling:

- **Show, Don't Tell:** Instead of simply stating facts, recreate scenes and emotions. Describe the sensory details of moments—the colors, sounds, and smells—that invite readers to experience the event with you.
- **Character Development:** Even though this is your memoir, each person who played a significant role in your life is a character in your story. Portray them deeply, including their personalities, actions, and influences on your life.
- **Setting Scenes:** Each scene in your memoir helps build the world you lived in. Describe settings vividly to transport readers to the place and time where your stories unfolded.

Publishing Options

Once your memoir is written, consider how you want to share it. Traditional publishing is an option if you're interested in a broader distribution, though it can be a challenging and lengthy process. Self-publishing, on the other hand, offers more control and quicker turnaround. Platforms like Amazon's Kindle Direct Publishing allow you to publish your memoir digitally and in print, making it easy to share with family and friends. Additionally, consider digitizing your memoirs—creating audio or electronic versions that can be easily shared or accessed online.

Interactive Element: Memoir Writing Prompt

- **Reflective Writing Exercise:** Think about an event that significantly changed your perspective on life. Write a detailed description of the event, focusing on your thoughts and feelings, how you reacted, and what you learned. This exercise can be a building block for a chapter in your memoir.

Writing your memoirs is not just about preserving the past; it's about sharing your journey's wisdom and touching the lives of others with your story. As you embark on this writing adventure, remember that each word you pen is a legacy, a gift to the future that offers insight, inspiration, and connection.

Crafting: From Beginner Projects to Advanced Techniques

Imagine a quiet afternoon with the sun streaming through the window, a perfect setting to sit at a crafting table with colorful yarns, clay, or scrapbook materials in front of you. Crafting isn't just a hobby; it's a journey into creativity, offering a spectrum of activities that range from knitting and pottery to scrapbooking and woodworking. Each craft invites you to dive into a world of color, texture, and form, engaging your hands and mind in creating something truly personal and unique.

Let's start with knitting, a wonderful entry point into the crafting world due to its relatively simple tools and techniques. All you need is a pair of knitting needles and some yarn. Beginners can start with basic stitches, creating simple projects like scarves or coasters, which provide immediate satisfaction and a sense of accomplishment. As your skills grow, you might venture into more complex patterns like hats, sweaters, or even intricate lacework, challenging your dexterity and enhancing your ability to follow detailed instructions and patterns.

On the other hand, pottery offers a tactile experience that engages your sense of touch and artistic instincts. Starting with a lump of clay, you can explore basic hand-building techniques like pinching, coiling, and slab construction to create functional items such as bowls, vases, or plates. For those intrigued by the pottery wheel, local community centers or art schools often offer classes that provide guided instruction and the necessary equipment. The magic of transforming a piece of earth into a polished, glazed, and fired piece of art provides a profound connection to the material and the creative process.

Scrapbooking is another craft that preserves memories and allows you to express your narrative style. It involves arranging photographs, memorabilia, and embellishments in a decorative album, turning a simple collection of photos into a storybook of your life's moments. Beginners can start with basic layouts, learning how to balance colors, textures, and typography to enhance the visual appeal of their pages. Advanced scrapbookers might delve into digital scrapbooking, using software to create digital pages that can be printed, shared online, or transformed into multimedia presentations.

Woodworking combines the beauty of natural materials with the satisfaction of building something sturdy and functional. Simple projects like birdhouses or picture frames introduce basic skills such as measuring, cutting, and assembling. These projects can be completed with minimal tools, making them accessible for beginners. More advanced projects, like furniture making or intricate carving, require more specialized tools and techniques but offer the reward of creating heirloom-quality pieces that can be cherished for generations.

Crafting Communities and Mental Health Benefits

Joining a crafting group or community can significantly enhance the enjoyment and benefits of your crafting endeavors. These groups provide a space to share techniques, exchange ideas, and socialize with others who share your interests. Many community centers, libraries, and even cafes host crafting circles that welcome participants of all skill levels. Online communities and forums offer vast resources to connect with crafters worldwide, participate in challenges, and find inspiration for new projects.

The mental health benefits of crafting are notable. Engaging in crafts can act as a form of meditation, allowing you to focus on the task while setting aside worries and stressors. The repetitive motions involved in knitting or the focused attention required in pottery can induce a calm, meditative state, reducing anxiety and promoting a sense of peace. Moreover, creating something tangible boosts self-esteem and provides a tangible measure of progress and accomplishment. Whether crafting alone or as part of a group, making something with your hands can be incredibly therapeutic and fulfilling.

Crafting offers a unique blend of creative expression, skill development, and mental relaxation. It allows you to explore new materials and techniques, express your vision, and connect with a community of like-minded individuals. Whether you are a beginner looking to learn a new skill or an experienced crafter seeking to master your art, crafting provides endless opportunities for personal growth and enjoyment.

Engaging with Digital Media Creation

Stepping into the world of digital media creation can open a window to a breeze of endless possibilities. It's a space where technology meets creativity, allowing you to capture, enhance, and share experiences from your unique perspective. Whether through digital photography, video production, or graphic design, the digital tools available offer ways to turn ideas into visual stories that resonate and inspire. For many seniors, navigating these technologies might seem daunting at first. Still, with the right guidance and tools, it can become manageable and an enriching way to express your creativity and connect with others.

Let's begin with digital photography, an excellent entry point into digital media. Unlike traditional photography, digital cameras and smartphones offer immediate feedback through their screens, allowing you to see the results instantly and make adjustments as needed. The basic equipment—a digital camera or a smartphone—is likely already part of your daily life. Understanding the settings like exposure, light, and angles can greatly enhance the quality of your photos. Online platforms such as YouTube and Udemy offer beginner-friendly tutorials that explain these concepts in simple terms, often with visual demonstrations that make learning engaging and effective.

Venturing into video production opens another exciting chapter. Creating videos can be as simple as using your smartphone to capture moments from family gatherings or as intricate as producing a documentary about a topic you're passionate about. Basic video editing software like iMovie for Mac users or Windows Movie Maker for PC users provides user-friendly interfaces. These programs allow you to cut footage, add transitions, and insert text or music, giving life to your videos. For those who want to dive deeper, classes offered by local community centers or online courses can provide more advanced skills and techniques.

Graphic design might sound like it's only for professionals, but it's quite accessible with today's intuitive software. Tools like Canva and Adobe Spark offer free versions and ready-made templates for creating everything from greeting cards to digital photo albums. These platforms are designed with ease of use in mind, making it possible for you to drag and drop elements, mix fonts and colors, and create beautiful designs without any previous experience.

Creative Projects to Start With

Imagine turning your photos into a beautiful collage or crafting custom greeting cards for friends and family. These projects allow you to apply your new skills and create personalized gifts that carry a piece of your creativity. Online tutorials can guide you step by step through these projects, ensuring you have support at every stage. Additionally, creating a simple video documentary about a family event or a personal hobby can be a fulfilling project that not only documents important moments but also hones your storytelling skills through multimedia.

Sharing and Marketing Digital Creations

Once you're ready to share your creations, the digital world offers platforms far beyond your immediate circle. For instance, Etsy provides a marketplace for selling digital art, allowing you to reach customers worldwide. Similarly, platforms like YouTube are perfect for sharing videos, whether personal vlogs, educational content, or creative storytelling. Blogs and social media platforms like Instagram and Pinterest are also excellent for showcasing your digital photography and graphic designs, helping you connect with like-minded individuals who appreciate and inspire your work.

In engaging with digital media creation, you're doing more than just keeping up with technology; you're actively participating in modern expression that connects across generations and geographies. This venture into digital creativity is more than just learning to use tools; it's about embracing a medium that allows for continuous learning and sharing—a way to leave a digital footprint that is uniquely yours.

As this chapter closes, we reflect on the transformative power of digital media in expressing and sharing your creative vision. From capturing the perfect photograph to producing a heartfelt video or designing a unique piece of digital art, the skills you develop can enrich your life and the lives of others. These endeavors keep you connected to the modern world and provide a fulfilling outlet for creativity and personal expression. Looking ahead, the next chapter will navigate the nuances of community involvement and leadership in retirement, exploring how you can use your newfound skills and experiences to influence and inspire your community.

THIRTEEN

Community Involvement and Leadership

I magine a crisp morning in your hometown. The streets are quiet, but the promise of activity hums in the air as young and old community members gather at the local park. Today, they're coming together to plant a garden, an initiative you helped bring to life. This isn't just about beautifying the area—it's a project that knits the community closer, fosters new friendships, and bridges the gap between generations. You're at the heart of this movement, a testament to the vital role seniors can play in invigorating and leading community projects. This chapter is dedicated to guiding you through the rewarding process of leading community initiatives, from the spark of an idea to the ongoing flame of its impact.

Leading Community Initiatives for Seniors

Identifying Community Needs

The first step in becoming a community leader is recognizing where your leadership is most needed. Your unique position as a senior grants you a broad perspective, one that combines historical insights with contemporary concerns. Start by engaging with your community to pinpoint gaps and opportunities where your involvement could make a significant difference. Hold informal gatherings, perhaps over coffee or at a local meeting hall, where community members can voice concerns and pitch ideas. Tools like community surveys, accessible online and in paper format, can help collect more structured feedback. These interactions can be eye-opening, highlighting issues ranging from more accessible park benches to programs that engage local youth in positive activities.

Establishing Community Projects

Once you've identified a community need, the next step is to lay the groundwork for a project that addresses it. Effective community projects require clear goals, planned logistics, and a lot of passion. Let's say the issue is an increase in neighborhood crime. A neighborhood watch program could be the answer, enhancing safety and fostering community solidarity. Begin by outlining the project's scope: What areas will it cover? Who will be involved? What are the expected outcomes? Then, move on to the resources needed—like volunteer patrols, coordination with local police, and community awareness campaigns. Leadership here means being the linchpin that brings these elements together, organizing meetings to discuss roles and responsibilities, and ensuring a solid plan.

Building a Volunteer Team

No leader can handle a community project alone, and here's where your skills in building and managing a volunteer team come in. Recruiting volunteers requires understanding what motivates people—some might be driven by social interaction, others by the desire to give back, and others by the need to build their resumes. Appeal to these motivations in your recruitment efforts, and provide clear information about the commitments and benefits involved. Managing your team effectively means recognizing the strengths of different members and delegating tasks accordingly. Perhaps more importantly, it involves fostering a sense of community and appreciation among your volunteers. Regular thank-you notes, recognition events, and feedback sessions help maintain enthusiasm and commitment.

Sustaining Initiatives

The longevity of a community project depends on careful planning and adaptability. Securing funding can be challenging, but many communities have local grants sponsored by businesses or government agencies that support civic projects. Documenting processes and progress is crucial for reporting to stakeholders and evaluating what works and doesn't, allowing for necessary adjustments. Training successors is also an essential part of sustainability. As a senior, part of your legacy can be mentoring younger community members to take over leadership roles, ensuring the project thrives beyond your active involvement.

Interactive Element: Community Project Planner

To help you get started, here's a simple planner tool:

- **Goal:** Define what you aim to achieve.
- **Needs Assessment:** List the steps you'll take to identify community needs (surveys, meetings).

- **Resources Required:** Detail what resources (people, money, materials) will be needed.
- **Team Roles:** Outline potential volunteer roles and the skills required for each.
- **Timeline:** Set a timeline for initial milestones.

Leading community initiatives offers a powerful way for seniors like you to contribute significantly to society, leveraging your life experiences and knowledge to benefit others. It's about making a tangible difference, leaving a legacy of active citizenship that could inspire future generations. As you move forward, remember that each small step contributes to a larger journey that enhances your community and enriches your life with purpose and connection.

Advocating for Senior Rights and Needs

Advocacy is much like being a voice for those who might not be heard, a champion for the rights and needs crucial for a dignified life. As seniors, embracing advocacy means taking an active role in shaping the policies and services that affect your life and the lives of your peers. It's about ensuring that older adults' collective wisdom and challenges are acknowledged and addressed publicly. Advocacy can take many forms, from penning impactful letters to legislators, making your voices heard at town hall meetings, and joining forces with senior advocacy groups pushing for systemic change.

The issues that touch on the lives of seniors are as diverse as they are critical. Healthcare, for instance, is a major area of concern, encompassing everything from Medicare coverage and prescription drug costs to long-term care and mental health services. Housing, too, is a significant issue, as many seniors face challenges related to affordability, accessibility, and suitability of their living conditions as they age. Then there's the broad category of essential services, which includes transportation, senior-specific recreation, and access to nutritious food. Understanding these issues deeply helps craft arguments and solutions that resonate with policymakers and the community, ensuring that the solutions developed are practical and empathetic to the unique challenges faced by the aging population.

Engaging effectively with policymakers is a skill that can be honed over time. Start by identifying the local, state, and national representatives who have the power to influence senior-related policies. Crafting clear, concise, and compelling messages to these policymakers is crucial. Whether through writing letters, making phone calls, or scheduling meetings, your communications should always state the issue clearly, explain how it affects you and your peers, and propose a solution or request specific action. Participating in public hearings and forums is another powerful way to influence policy. These forums offer a platform to speak directly to decision-makers and to make your case in front of an audience, potentially swaying public opinion and gaining broader support for your cause.

Social media has become a formidable tool in advocacy, allowing messages to reach far beyond traditional community boundaries. Platforms like Facebook, Twitter, and Instagram can amplify your voice, helping to rally support, spread awareness, and even organize collective actions like petitions or protests. However, the key to successful online advocacy is maintaining a respectful and factual tone, encouraging engagement and fostering constructive discussions.

In advocacy, there's strength in numbers, and leveraging existing networks can significantly amplify your efforts. Collaborating with established organizations with a track record in senior advocacy can provide access to resources, expertise, and a larger audience. These partnerships can lead to more impactful campaigns, as combined efforts often draw more attention and resources, increasing the chances of achieving substantial changes. Moreover, working within a network can provide moral support and a sense of solidarity, which is invaluable in sustaining long-term advocacy efforts.

In essence, becoming an advocate for your rights and needs is not just about fighting for what you deserve; it's about contributing to a society that respects and values its elders. It's about ensuring that senior voices are heard and a driving force behind meaningful changes. Through advocacy, you can shape a world that meets the needs of today's seniors and sets the foundation for future generations as they reach their golden years.

Organizing Local Events for Broader Engagement

Imagine the buzz and excitement of a local fair, where everyone from toddlers to grandparents gathers, sharing smiles and stories. Organizing such community events can be fulfilling, enhancing the social fabric and bringing joy to many. Events like health fairs, educational workshops, and cultural celebrations don't just happen; they result from careful planning and enthusiastic execution. Let's walk through the essentials of event planning tailored specifically for community-oriented gatherings.

Starting with the basics, setting clear objectives is the first step in planning any event. What do you hope to achieve? Is it to educate, celebrate, or raise awareness about a local cause? Once your goals are crystal clear, you can outline the who, what, when, where, and how. Budgeting comes next; detailing every potential expense is crucial to avoid surprises. This includes costs for venue rentals, supplies, entertainment, and refreshments. Securing sponsorships from local businesses can help manage these costs while building stronger community ties.

Selecting the right venue is paramount and goes hand-in-hand with your event objectives. For a health fair, you might need space for booths and private areas for health screenings. A local community center with audio-visual facilities would be ideal for a workshop. Accessibility is key; ensure the venue is accessible to everyone, including those with mobility challenges. Promoting your event effectively ensures that the community knows about it and is excited to participate. Utilize local newspapers, community bulletin boards, social media, and word of mouth to spread the word. Engaging local influencers or respected community members to endorse or speak at your event can boost visibility and attendance.

Making your event enjoyable and accessible for all attendees, regardless of age or mobility, involves thoughtful planning. Ensure there are ample seating and rest areas and that restrooms are accessible. Transportation might be a barrier for some community members, so consider arranging transportation options or providing clear information on public transport links to the venue. For families, having a dedicated kids' zone can keep younger ones entertained while adults participate in the main activities. Diverse programming that resonates with different interests and cultural backgrounds also enriches the experience, ensuring everyone finds something valuable and enjoyable at your event.

Technology can significantly enhance the event experience and streamline management tasks. Online registration tools simplify the process for attendees and provide organizers with valuable data on participant numbers and preferences. During the event, live streaming can bring the experience to those unable to attend in person, broadening your reach. Apps designed for events can offer interactive features such as schedules, maps, and feedback forms, making the experience smoother and more engaging for participants. After the event, gathering feedback is crucial to gauge success and identify areas for improvement. Online surveys, direct feedback forms, and informal conversations during the event can all provide insights into what worked well and what could be enhanced.

Evaluating the success of your event involves looking at both quantitative and qualitative data. How many attended? Did you meet your financial goals? What was the overall satisfaction rate? These metrics are invaluable for planning future events. They tell you if you met your goals and how the event impacted the community. This ongoing evaluation informs your future efforts, ensuring that each event is more successful and impactful than the last.

In organizing local events, you're doing more than just bringing people together. You're creating opportunities for learning, celebration, and connection, enriching your community's social and cultural landscape. Each successful event builds your confidence and skills as an organizer, contributing to a vibrant, engaged community that values and supports its members across all generations.

As this chapter closes, we reflect on the powerful role that well-planned and inclusive community events play in enhancing the lives of all community members. They foster a sense of belonging, promote understanding and cooperation, and celebrate the diverse experiences and cultures within the community. The next chapter will explore the essentials of navigating the healthcare system, ensuring you and your peers are well-informed and prepared to manage your health confidently.

FOURTEEN

Navigating the Healthcare System

Picture a calm afternoon, perhaps in your favorite part of the home, with the sunlight gently filtering through. A sense of peace comes from knowing you're well-prepared for anything the day might bring. This same tranquility can extend to understanding and navigating your healthcare options as you age, particularly regarding Medicare. Think of this chapter as a friendly guide through the maze of Medicare, designed to help you make informed decisions that ensure your health needs are met without unnecessary stress.

Understanding Your Medicare Options

Embarking on the Medicare journey can feel daunting with its various parts and plans, each with its own rules and benefits. Let's simplify it together. Medicare is split into four main parts: A, B, C, and D. Each part covers different aspects of your healthcare needs, and understanding these differences is crucial for choosing the best options for your health and financial well-being.

Medicare Part A and Part B are often referred to as Original Medicare. Part A covers your hospital stays, care in a skilled nursing facility, hospice care, and home health care services. It's like a safety net for those significant, less frequent health care services. Part A comes without a monthly premium for most of you, provided you or your spouse paid Medicare taxes while working.

Part B covers routine medical expenses, such as doctor's visits, outpatient care, preventive services, and supplies. Unlike Part A, Part B comes with a monthly premium. Think of it as your standard health insurance coverage, handling those regular, necessary check-ups and treatments that keep you ticking along.

Medicare Part C, also known as Medicare Advantage, is slightly different. Offered by private insurance companies approved by Medicare, these plans bundle Part A and Part B and often include Part D, which covers prescription drugs. These plans can offer additional benefits like vision, hearing, and dental care, which aren't covered under Original Medicare. Think of Part C as an all-in-one package that might simplify your healthcare but requires you to use doctors and facilities that are part of the plan's network.

Medicare Part D adds prescription drug coverage to your Original Medicare benefits, which is essential since neither Part A nor B covers most prescriptions. With the rising cost of medications, having Part D can be a financial relief. Each Part D plan has its list of covered drugs, known as a formulary, so you'll need to ensure your prescriptions are covered under your chosen plan.

Navigating the enrollment process is another vital piece of the puzzle. You have a 7-month Initial Enrollment Period around your 65th birthday to sign up for Medicare, starting three months before the month you turn 65 and ending three months after. Missing this window could mean penalties and delayed coverage, so it's crucial to mark this on your calendar.

For those weighing the benefits of Medicare Advantage versus Traditional Medicare, consider your health needs and financial situation. Medicare Advantage might offer more comprehensive coverage and lower out-of-pocket costs. However, it's less flexible regarding the providers you can see. Traditional Medicare, on the other hand, offers more freedom in choosing doctors and specialists but might have higher out-of-pocket costs and doesn't cover things like prescription drugs without Part D.

Supplemental Coverage Options

Understanding supplemental coverage options, such as Medigap, is like having an umbrella in a rainstorm—it's not essential, but it sure is helpful. Private companies sell Medigap policies and can cover copayments, deductibles, and healthcare if you travel outside the U.S., which Medicare doesn't cover. These policies can only be used with Original Medicare, not Medicare Advantage. Exploring Medigap might be wise if you opt for Original Medicare and want the extra security of knowing unexpected costs will be covered.

Navigating your Medicare options isn't just about finding the right coverage—it's about ensuring peace of mind. It's about making informed decisions that allow you to enjoy your retirement without undue worry about healthcare. Whether you're gathering documents to enroll, comparing the pros and cons of different Medicare plans, or considering additional coverage like Medigap, remember that this process is about securing your health and happiness. By understanding your options, you can choose the best path for your healthcare needs, ensuring you're covered no matter what life throws your way.

Choosing the Right Healthcare Providers

When selecting healthcare providers, think of it as forming your healthcare team, where each member brings unique skills tailored precisely to your needs. This team is your frontline defense in maintaining your health, so choosing the right professionals is crucial. The criteria for selecting these providers go beyond their credentials and experience; they involve a mix of their specialization, experience with senior health issues, geographical accessibility, and, importantly, their compatibility with Medicare.

Firstly, consider the specialties you require. For instance, a cardiologist might become as crucial as a general practitioner as we age, especially if heart-related issues are common in your family history. Similarly, the need for a geriatrician specializing in older adults' care might arise, offering expertise in the unique health issues that affect seniors. These professionals provide treatment and preventive care advice tailored to more mature needs. Their role can be pivotal in managing chronic conditions such as arthritis or diabetes, ensuring that such conditions do not prevent you from enjoying life to the fullest.

The location of healthcare providers is another vital factor. Proximity and ease of access can significantly influence your regularity of visits. A provider who is a short drive away—or better yet, accessible via public transportation—ensures that attending appointments is less chore, especially when you might not feel up to a long commute. Furthermore, this proximity can be invaluable in urgent health needs, providing quick access to care when it matters most.

Compatibility with Medicare is non-negotiable. Not all doctors accept Medicare, so confirming that a provider is part of the Medicare program should be one of your initial steps before finalizing your choice. This ensures that the financial aspects of your care are predictable and managed, avoiding unexpected out-of-pocket expenses that could disrupt your budget and peace of mind.

Building a Healthcare Team

Having a coordinated care team is like having a symphony orchestra, where each member plays a distinct part but creates a harmonious sound together. This team might include your primary care physician, various specialists, and healthcare professionals like nutritionists or physical therapists. Each one plays a specific role, addressing different aspects of your health, from diet to mobility, chronic condition management, and preventive care.

The central figure in this team is usually your primary care physician. They are like a conductor, overseeing your health care, coordinating with specialists, and keeping track of your overall health progress. They are your go-to for most health concerns and can guide you on preventive care practices to keep you in your best shape. From there, specialists focus on specific organs or systems when issues that require more detailed attention arise. At the same time, allied health professionals like dieticians or physical therapists help manage and improve your daily functioning and quality of life.

Integrating their efforts can lead to better health outcomes. For example, if you're managing diabetes, your endocrinologist might adjust your medication, your dietician can tailor your diet to control your blood sugar levels better, and your primary care physician can monitor your overall health markers. This coordinated approach ensures that all aspects of your condition are managed effectively, reducing the risk of complications and improving your quality of life.

Using Technology to Find and Assess Providers

Finding and assessing healthcare providers has always been challenging in today's digital age. Various online tools and resources can aid in this process. Websites like Healthgrades or ZocDoc allow you to search for doctors by specialty and location while providing patient reviews that can give you insights into others' experiences with the provider. These platforms often include detailed profiles of doctors, including their education, certifications, and areas of expertise, helping you make an informed decision.

Moreover, Medicare offers tools to compare doctors, hospitals, and other providers based on quality ratings, distance, and services. This can be particularly helpful if you're considering Medicare Advantage plans and need to check if your preferred providers are in-network.

Changing Providers

Sometimes, despite careful selection, you may find that a provider needs to match your needs. Changing healthcare providers is a decision that can feel as significant as starting a new relationship—it requires thought and, sometimes, courage. When the change is necessary, gather your medical records, which you can obtain anytime. Most clinics and hospitals now offer electronic health records that you can access online, making this process easier.

When choosing a new provider, communicate openly about your medical history and health goals. This open dialogue is crucial in building a trustful and effective relationship. Remember, this team's goal is to keep you healthy and thriving, and sometimes, finding the right team members takes a bit of trial and adjustment.

Navigating the healthcare landscape requires thoughtfulness and proactive decision-making. Still, with the right tools and information, you can assemble a healthcare team that feels less like an assortment of specialists and more like a circle of trusted advisors. This team is your partner in the journey toward sustained health and vitality, enabling you to embrace your senior years with confidence and peace.

Preventive Care Strategies to Keep You Healthy

Imagine the gentle care with which one tends to a beloved garden, nurturing it to bloom with vibrant health and vitality. This nurturing is much like the preventive care we give to our bodies, an essential practice that helps us flourish throughout our golden years. Engaging proactively with preventive healthcare is foundational to staving off diseases and living our retirement years with minimal disruptions and maximal joy. Discuss how embracing preventive care can significantly enhance your well-being and how Medicare supports these efforts.

Preventive care encompasses a range of services and practices to prevent illnesses before they start or catch health issues early when they are most treatable. Medicare recognizes the importance of this proactive approach and covers various preventive services and screenings at no cost to you, provided you see doctors who accept assignments in Medicare. This coverage includes annual wellness visits, where you can discuss your health status and risks with your doctor and develop a personalized prevention plan. Reviewing your family and personal health history during these visits is crucial, as it can provide vital clues about risk factors for diseases like diabetes, heart disease, or cancer.

Routine screenings are a cornerstone of preventive care, and for good reason. Screenings such as mammograms for breast cancer, colonoscopies for colorectal cancer, and bone density tests for osteoporosis can detect diseases in their nascent stages, often before you even show symptoms. These screenings are not arbitrary; they are backed by extensive research and are recommended based on factors like age, gender, and medical history. For instance, women over 65 are advised to have a bone density test to check for osteoporosis, while both men and women are recommended to get colorectal screenings starting at age 50. Immunizations, too, play a critical role and are fully covered under Medicare Part B. Vaccinations for influenza, pneumococcal pneumonia, and Hepatitis B are recommended for seniors, as these diseases can have severe implications as we age.

Beyond these screenings and vaccinations, the role of lifestyle factors in preventive health cannot be overstated. Choices about diet, exercise, smoking, and sleep profoundly impact health. A balanced diet rich in fruits, vegetables, lean proteins, and whole grains can help manage weight, reduce the risk of chronic diseases like type 2 diabetes, and support overall vitality. Regular physical activity keeps your body strong and your joints flexible, reduces the risk of heart disease, and can improve your mood and energy levels. If you smoke, quitting is perhaps one of the most powerful steps you can take for your health, significantly reducing the risk of lung cancer and heart disease. Adequate sleep, too, plays a critical role in health, impacting everything from cognitive function and energy levels to metabolic health and immune function.

Chronic conditions such as diabetes, hypertension, and heart disease require vigilant management to prevent complications. Regular monitoring of blood pressure, blood sugar levels, and cholesterol, combined with medications as prescribed, can keep these conditions under control and prevent them from escalating into more serious health issues. Engaging with your healthcare team to regularly review and adjust your treatment plans and being diligent about taking medications correctly are key elements of effective management. Additionally, lifestyle adjustments such as reducing sodium intake, increasing physical activity, and monitoring carbohydrate intake can complement medical treatments and improve health outcomes.

Preventive care is essentially about making wise choices today that will pay dividends in the future—like investing in your health bank to withdraw a life full of vigor and vitality later. By participating actively in your preventive care, staying informed about the screenings and services available, and making lifestyle choices that support your long-term health, you are setting the stage for a vibrant, active retirement. Embrace these practices not just as medical advice but as integral parts of your daily life, knowing that each healthy choice contributes to a fuller, more joyful experience in your later years.

FIFTEEN

Embracing the Golden Years

Imagine sitting comfortably in your favorite chair, perhaps with a cup of tea in hand, watching the golden hues of sunset spill through the window. It's moments like these—quiet, reflective, beautifully ordinary—that remind us of the grace found in the art of aging. As we traverse this chapter together, think of it as a gentle stroll through a garden of wisdom, where each step reveals new ways to embrace the changes that come with aging, not just with acceptance but with a heart full of positivity.

The Art of Aging Gracefully

Embracing changes with positivity isn't just about making the best of where you are now; it's about transforming your perspective to see new opportunities in every alteration life brings. As your physical capabilities evolve and your lifestyle shifts, viewing these changes through a lens of positivity can profoundly impact your overall well-being and happiness. It's like a gardener who prunes a beloved rose bush; though it seems drastic, the pruning enhances the plant's future bloom. Similarly, embracing changes in your life can lead to new paths and experiences.

Maintaining an active lifestyle is crucial as it intertwines with your physical and mental health. Staying active doesn't necessarily mean engaging in strenuous activities; it encompasses any joyful movement that suits your current physical state. For instance, gardening can be a serene way to stay active, or perhaps morning walks through your neighborhood. These activities keep your body moving and can significantly boost your mood and mental sharpness. The key is finding activities you look forward to, transforming exercise from a chore into a cherished part of your day.

Let's talk about beauty and self-care routines. Aging gracefully isn't about denying the aging process but embracing it with care and love. Adapting your beauty routines to enhance your comfort and self-appreciation is important. This might mean swapping out an old skincare routine for one that focuses on hydration and protection or perhaps embracing your natural hair color with a new style that feels both refreshing and reaffirming. Self-care is a profound expression of self-respect; by adapting your routines, you're honoring the person you've become.

Role Models Who Inspire

Consider the stories of individuals who embody the essence of aging gracefully. Take, for instance, the renowned actress Helen Mirren, who champions a life of activity and advocacy, showing that age is not a barrier to vibrancy and influence. Or think of the late author and poet Maya Angelou, who embraced each year of her life with renewed vigor, her wisdom deepening with time, reflecting her belief in the value of experience and the beauty of growing older. These role models don't just live; they thrive, their lives rich with pursuits that inspire both themselves and others.

Each element—positivity, activity, self-care, and inspiring role models—creates a fulfilling and enjoyable aging experience. Embracing this approach means navigating life's changes with resilience and joy, appreciating the beauty in every phase. This chapter reminds us that aging isn't just about reflecting on the past and looking forward to each new day's opportunities.

Keeping Your Spiritual Life Enriched

Imagine the early morning stillness, the world just waking up, and you, seated quietly, feeling the peace that comes with a meditative start to your day. This quiet, reflective practice is one of many spiritual activities that can enrich your later years, bringing a depth of peace and understanding that often comes with life's experiences—exploring various spiritual practices, whether meditation, prayer, tai chi, or yoga, opens up a wellspring of emotional and spiritual well-being that can support you through aging.

Meditation, for instance, allows you to cultivate a state of mindfulness, which can help you navigate the ebb and flow of daily life with greater composure. It teaches you to live in the moment, appreciating each breath and each day as a unique gift. Whether traditional or conversational, prayer offers a deep connection to a higher power, providing comfort, guidance, and a sense of belonging to something greater. Tai chi and yoga blend physical movement with spiritual focus, enhancing flexibility, mental clarity, and emotional resilience.

The benefits of these practices are manifold; they help reduce stress, improve sleep patterns, lower blood pressure, and enhance overall well-being. However, one of the most significant benefits is the sense of community they can foster. Engaging in these practices can connect you with groups of like-minded individuals on their paths of spiritual discovery. Whether they meet in local parks, churches, temples, or online, these communities can offer support and fellowship, enriching your spiritual journey.

Finding Spiritual Communities

To find these communities, start by checking local community boards, libraries, or online platforms where groups often post meeting times and types of activities. Many community centers offer yoga or tai chi classes, which help you stay physically active and connect with others in your age group. Online platforms provide access to a global community where you can share experiences and insights and even participate in virtual classes and prayer groups, which is particularly helpful if mobility is an issue.

Exploring spiritual growth isn't limited to physical or communal activities; it also extends into literature and the arts, which can be profound sources of inspiration and contemplation. Reading books that delve into spiritual themes or listening to music that soothes the soul can be just as enriching as any physical practice. For those who enjoy visual arts, visiting galleries or painting can be a way to explore and express spiritual concepts and emotions visually.

Spiritual Growth Through Literature and Arts

Consider incorporating books like "The Book of Joy" by the Dalai Lama and Desmond Tutu or "Falling Upward" by Richard Rohr into your reading list. These books offer deep insights into the nature of spiritual growth and happiness from different cultural and religious perspectives. Music, too, can be a powerful medium for spiritual exploration. Listening to classical composers like Bach or modern meditative music can elevate your mood and spirit.

Keeping a spiritual journal or creating art that reflects your spiritual experiences can be incredibly fulfilling. These activities allow you to express your spiritual journey in tangible forms and serve as a personal reflection of your growth. A journal can be a private, sacred space where you document thoughts, feelings, and revelations along your spiritual path. At the same time, art can be a public expression of your inner world, shared with others to inspire and communicate deeper truths.

Documenting your spiritual journey through writing, painting, or any other creative expression helps solidify and clarify your experiences. It reminds you how far you've come and can guide others on similar paths.

Leaving a Legacy Through Community Service

As the chapters of your life unfold, the stories written in each carry a wealth of knowledge and lessons that can illuminate paths for you and others embarking on their own life's journeys. Community service is not just an avenue for giving back; it's a powerful means of sharing your life's narrative, impacting lives beyond your immediate circle, and crafting a legacy that resonates through generations. Let's explore how you can channel your passions and experiences into community service, creating a ripple effect that enhances the lives of others and provides profound personal fulfillment.

Identifying personal causes and passions can sometimes feel like finding a familiar tune within a symphony. Start by reflecting on the moments when you felt most engaged and alive. What were you doing? Who were you helping? Whether it was a professional accomplishment or a personal interest that sparked that joy, these are clues to your passions. For many, this might be environmental conservation, education, or arts and culture. Once identified, these causes can become the cornerstones of your community service efforts, guiding you toward activities and organizations where your contributions will have the most impact. For instance, if education is your passion, consider contacting local schools to see how you can contribute, perhaps by aiding in reading programs or sharing your professional expertise in career talks.

Mentorship offers a direct line to share your knowledge and wisdom with individuals just starting or looking to grow in your former field. The benefits of becoming a mentor are manifold; you get to impart your hard-earned wisdom and stay engaged with current developments in your field, keeping your skills sharp. It's a two-way street where your insights help shape someone's career or personal development, and their fresh perspectives can invigorate your understanding and appreciation of your field. Consider connecting with local universities, professional associations, or online platforms that facilitate mentorship. Share not just your technical know-how but the life lessons that helped you navigate the challenges and triumphs of your career.

Creating a Charitable Fund or Scholarship

Setting up a charitable fund or scholarship can be one of the most enduring ways to ensure your passion supports future generations. Begin by deciding the focus of your fund or scholarship. Will it support local students and researchers in a specific field or provide resources for community arts programs? Once the focus is clear, consulting with a financial advisor or an attorney can help you understand the options for funding and structuring your initiative. Community foundations can be excellent partners in this endeavor, as they often handle the administrative burden, allowing you to focus on the fund's impact. When setting up the fund, consider involving family members or close colleagues who share your vision—they can help ensure the fund's purpose is preserved and contribute to its growth over time.

Sharing your life lessons and wisdom can be as simple as telling your story. Public speaking, writing articles, or hosting workshops are all powerful platforms for reaching others. Local clubs, schools, and libraries often seek guest speakers or workshop leaders who can provide valuable insights on various topics. Whether it's a talk on the lessons learned from your career, a workshop on practical skills like budgeting or creative writing, or an article series in a community newsletter, these contributions enrich the community's knowledge and inspire others to learn and grow. In sharing your story, focus on the challenges overcome and the wisdom gained, providing a roadmap for success and showing the resilience and adaptability crucial at every stage of life.

You build a legacy that enriches your community meaningfully and enduringly by engaging in service, mentorship, philanthropy, and sharing. Each act of service and lesson shared contributes to a narrative of generosity and growth, impacting lives and stories yet to unfold.

Finding Joy in Everyday Moments

In everyday life, each moment holds the potential for joy and discovery if we take the time to notice and appreciate it. Embracing mindfulness is like opening a window in a room that's been closed off too long; it invites light, fresh air, and a new perspective into our daily routines. Mindfulness, the art of being present at the moment, can transform mundane activities into sources of joy and contentment. It's about noticing the sun's warmth on your skin, the laughter of children playing in the park, or the intricate pattern of frost on your window.

Let's explore some simple mindfulness exercises you can weave into your daily life. For instance, try the 'Five Senses' exercise during your morning coffee. Focus on the coffee's aroma, the cup's warmth in your hands, the taste of each sip, the sounds around you, and the sight of the morning light. This practice enhances your enjoyment of the moment and grounds you in the 'here and now,' reducing stress and fostering a greater appreciation for small pleasures.

Celebrating small successes daily is another beautiful way to cultivate joy. Did you remember to water the plants? Did you make someone smile today? These are victories worth celebrating. Consider keeping a 'joy journal' where you jot down these successes and happy moments. Over time, this journal will become a treasure trove of positive memories that can lift your spirits on less sunny days. It's not just about recording events; it's about recognizing and valuing the small wins and the beauty they add to your life.

Engaging your senses fully can turn ordinary experiences into rich, enjoyable ones. For instance, when you eat, take it slow. Savor each bite and notice the textures, the flavors, and the smells. This makes the meal more enjoyable and aids digestion and satisfaction. Similarly, when you go for a walk, tune into the sounds of nature or the city, depending on where you are. Feel the breeze, watch the hustle and bustle or the sway of trees. Such practices enhance your sensory experiences and anchor you firmly in the present, making life feel fuller and more vibrant.

Engaging with Nature

Spending time in nature, whether tending to a garden, walking through a park, or simply sitting under a tree, can profoundly affect your psychological and physical well-being. Nature's inherent beauty and tranquility can help reduce stress, improve mood, and enhance physical well-being. Even in urban settings, connecting with nature can be as simple as visiting a local park, starting a container garden on a balcony, or setting up a bird feeder by a window to watch birds come and go. These connections remind us of the cycles of life and growth, echoing the changes and continuities in our lives.

These practices—mindfulness, celebrating small successes, engaging senses, and connecting with nature—are a gentle reminder that joy doesn't always come from grand gestures or significant achievements. Often, it's woven through the quiet, ordinary moments that fill our days, waiting to be discovered and cherished. As you go about your day, keep your eyes, ears, and heart open to these moments, and watch how they brighten your world, one small, beautiful detail at a time.

Reflecting on Achievements and Milestones

Imagine yourself sitting in a room filled with memorabilia, each marking a milestone from your rich life experiences. Creating a visual timeline of these milestones isn't just about reminiscing; it's a profound exercise in recognizing and celebrating the breadth of your achievements and the depth of your experiences. Think of this timeline as a personal museum exhibit showcasing the chapters of your life. Begin by gathering photos, souvenirs, and any keepsakes representing significant moments—your first job, family vacations, a major relocation, retirement parties, and everything in between. Arrange these items chronologically along a timeline crafted from a large piece of paper or digitally through apps that allow photo uploads and annotations. As you place each item, spend a moment reflecting on that period: what you learned, how you felt, and how it shaped the person you are today. This visual representation serves as a walk down memory lane and a vivid affirmation of your life's impact and evolution.

Celebration is integral to acknowledging your life's achievements. It's important to mark these milestones in ways that resonate personally. If you cherish intimacy, consider a small gathering with close friends and family where you can share stories and the significance of these achievements. For those who enjoy solitude, a personal retreat to a meaningful place can provide a serene environment to reflect and plan future adventures. Alternatively, organizing a community event that aligns with your achievements, such as a seminar if you're a retired educator or a showcase if you're an artist, can celebrate your milestones and inspire and educate others. These celebrations are personal affirmations, reminding you of your accomplishments and the varied capabilities you possess, each marked with joy and a sense of fulfillment.

Reflecting on past experiences is more than a nostalgic trip; it's a learning expedition where each event provides insights into decisions, consequences, and personal growth. Engaging in this reflection helps you understand the patterns of your life, the decisions that turned out to be pivotal, and areas where different choices have led to different outcomes. This isn't about regret but about learning and applying these lessons to current and future decisions. For instance, consider a major career decision you once made—what motivated this choice? What were the outcomes? Discussing these reflections with peers or mentors can provide new perspectives and deepen your understanding of life's complexities.

Sharing your stories with family and community cements your legacy and enriches listeners' lives, offering them resilience, adaptation, and success models. Your life's tales are a unique source of wisdom for younger generations, providing them with real-life illustrations of overcoming challenges and seizing opportunities. Organize storytelling sessions, perhaps during family gatherings or as part of community projects, where you can narrate your experiences, decisions, and the wisdom gained. These stories, woven from your personal and professional life, become invaluable lessons for others and a testament to your life's impact. This sharing creates a bond, a thread that connects your past with the future of others, fostering a deeper understanding and appreciation across generations. As you recount these stories, you'll find that they do not just pass on knowledge; they inspire, motivate, and resonate, continuing your influence and presence in the lives of others far beyond the confines of direct experience.

Planning for Major Life Transferences

In the story of your life, each event represents a time of change, some anticipated and others unexpected. As you navigate the later chapters of your life, the importance of planning for these transitions cannot be overstated. It's about setting the stage now for smoother changes later, whether they are changes in your health, living situations, or even the loss of a loved or cherished one. Think of this planning as preparing your boat before setting sail, ensuring it's equipped to handle whatever waters lie ahead.

Anticipating potential life changes involves a realistic assessment of what might be on your horizon. For instance, considering how you might handle a shift to a lower level of mobility or managing a chronic illness can help you put the necessary supports in place before they're needed. This might mean modifying your home to make it more accessible or researching home care services in your community. Similarly, the emotional impact of losing a partner or close friend is profound, and while it's not something we like to think about, considering how you'll cope and who you'll lean on can make the experience less overwhelming when it does happen. Engaging in open conversations with family and friends about these potential scenarios prepares you and them for future changes.

Legal and financial preparations form the backbone of your transition planning. Ensuring your will is current, setting up a living trust, and having advanced healthcare directives are crucial. These documents speak for you when you cannot, ensuring your wishes are respected and followed. For many, this might involve consulting with legal and financial advisors to ensure all paperwork reflects your current wishes and provides clear instructions for your estate. Additionally, it is essential to understand your financial landscape and how it will support you through various changes. This might mean setting aside funds for medical emergencies or long-term care needs.

Building and maintaining a strong support system is one of the most important aspects of planning for life transitions. This network, comprising family, friends, and professional advisors, is your anchor through any storm. They can offer practical help, like assisting with day-to-day needs or managing medical appointments, as well as emotional support, companionship and comfort during tough times. Cultivating these relationships now ensures that when changes occur, you're surrounded by a community that's informed, involved, and ready to support you. Consider regular check-ins with your network to keep them updated on your health and any changes in your living situation so they're not caught off-guard.

Emotional Resilience and Coping Strategies

Building emotional resilience is key to navigating major life changes. This involves developing coping strategies to face challenges with strength and grace. Stress management techniques such as mindfulness, deep breathing exercises, or yoga can significantly mitigate the emotional upheavals accompanying major transitions. Additionally, staying engaged with hobbies and interests that bring you joy can provide a much-needed outlet and sense of normalcy during change.

Professional counseling should be considered a resource. A therapist specializing in geriatric care can offer valuable guidance and support, helping you navigate your emotions and adjust to new life circumstances. They can also facilitate difficult family discussions, ensuring everyone is heard and that emotional undercurrents are addressed healthily.

Building a life imbued with emotional resilience prepares you to handle future transitions and enriches your everyday experiences, allowing you to face each day with optimism and strength.

As you continue crafting your life story, remember that each transition is another part of the vibrant narrative that defines you. With careful planning, a robust support system, and strategies for emotional resilience, you can approach these changes not as endings but as transformations—opportunities for growth and renewal. As this chapter of your life unfolds, take comfort in knowing that you are prepared, supported, and resilient, ready to embrace whatever comes your way with grace and strength.

Conclusion

As we draw the curtains on our shared journey through "The Ultimate Senior Retirement Guide," let's take a moment to reflect on the transformative path that retirement unfolds. From the initial steps beyond your career's end through exploring new identities and the vibrant possibilities that await in your golden years, this book has aimed to be your companion —supporting, guiding, and encouraging you every step of the way.

Together, we've navigated the emotional and practical shifts that retirement brings. We've stressed the importance of proactive health management, lifelong learning joy, and creative expression fulfillment. Each chapter was crafted to enrich your journey, showing how community involvement and personal growth are not just possible but essential pillars of a truly rewarding retirement.

We've discovered that change is an ever-present companion in our later years. Embracing it with resilience and positivity isn't just beneficial; it's crucial for thriving. Whether adapting to new health realities, adjusting living situations, or transforming social dynamics, your ability to flow with these changes determines the quality of your life as you age.

With all my heart, I encourage you to step into your retirement with courage and an open heart. See this not as a farewell to your working years but as a hello to freedom and opportunities that were once dreams. Let technology be your tool, a bridge to new hobbies, better health management, and staying connected with those you love.

Financial security and understanding your healthcare options are foundational to this new phase. We've covered how to navigate Medicare, select the right healthcare providers, and budget wisely to ensure you enjoy this period without financial worry.

Your potential to influence and shape your community remains undiminished. Through volunteer work, mentorship, or simply sharing your life's stories and wisdom, you have the power to leave a legacy that echoes through generations. And in the quieter moments, don't forget the importance of finding joy in the every day—the chirp of birds, the rustle of leaves, a book in your hands under the soft light of dawn.

As you turn each page of your life into this exciting chapter, I call on you to take the first step. Use the practical advice and inspirational guidance we've shared to craft a retirement that resonates with your deepest aspirations. You're not alone on this journey. Across the globe, many are navigating similar transitions, each with their fears and hopes and stories of endings and new beginnings.

Take a moment to ponder what a fulfilling retirement looks like for you. How will you use these days? What stories will you tell? The answers lie within you, ready to be discovered and lived.

Thank you for allowing me to be a part of your journey into retirement. Here's to your health, happiness, and a future brimming with possibilities. May your years ahead be as vibrant and rewarding as the chapters of your life that led you here.

Help Others Enjoy Their Golden Years

Now that you have everything you need to live a fulfilling retirement, it's time to share your newfound knowledge and help other readers discover the same joy.

Leaving your honest opinion of this book on Amazon will show other seniors where they can find the guidance they need to enjoy retirement.

Your review can:

- Help another retiree find purpose and joy.
- Show someone how to stay connected and active.
- Guide financial security in retirement.
- Inspire a new hobby or passion.
- Offer practical tips on health and wellness.

Simply scan the QR code below to leave your review:

Let's share the joy of retirement and inspire others. Your role in this journey is crucial, and I am deeply grateful for your help in making senior life fulfilling and exciting for all.

Your biggest fan,

Pauline Winslow

References

- *"Psychology Works" Fact Sheet: Retirement* https://cpa.ca/psychology-works-fact-sheet-retirement/
- *How to Set Retirement Goals and Where to Start* https://www.westernsouthern.com/retirement/how-to-set-retirement-goals
- *The Importance of a Daily Routine for Seniors* https://bluemoonseniorcounseling.com/the-importance-of-a-daily-routine-for-seniors/
- *Adjusting to Retirement: Handling Depression and Stress* https://www.helpguide.org/articles/aging-issues/adjusting-to-retirement.htm
- *7 Low Impact Exercises for Older Adults to Stay Active* https://www.humangood.org/resources/senior-living-blog/low-impact-exercises-for-older-adults
- *USDA MyPlate Nutrition Information for Older Adults* https://www.myplate.gov/life-stages/older-adults
- *14 Important Health Screenings for Older Adults* https://archwellhealth.com/news/14-important-health-screenings-for-older-adults/
- *Medication Management for Seniors: Tips From A Doctor* https://www.aplaceformom.com/caregiver-resources/articles/medication-management
- *6 Brain Exercises For Seniors To Try - Forbes* https://www.forbes.com/health/healthy-aging/brain-exercises/
- *Brain Stimulating Games and Cognitive Activities for Older ...* https://www.thecareside.com.au/post/brain-stimulating-games-and-cognitive-activities-for-older-adults/
- *Lifelong Learning in Retirement: Online Resources for ...* https://www.roadscholar.org/travel-tips/lifelong-learning-for-seniors/
- *40 Mental Health Resources for Seniors* https://www.seniorlifestyle.com/resources/blog/40-mental-health-resources-for-seniors/
- *The Importance of Gratitude for Senior Health | Ethos* https://www.ethoscare.org/news/the-benefits-of-gratitude-in-older-adults
- *Tips for older adults who are grieving* https://www.healthpartners.com/blog/grief-and-loss-in-older-adults/

- *The Theory Behind the Age-Related Positivity Effect - PMC* https://www.ncbi.nlm.nih.gov/pmc/articles/PMC3459016/
- *Why It's Important To Stay Social In Retirement And How ...* https://www.forbes.com/sites/robpascale/2019/10/31/staying-social-in-retirement/
- *Best Budgeting for Seniors in 2024* https://www.seniorliving.org/finance/budgeting-apps/
- *How to Plan for Medical Expenses in Retirement* https://www.investopedia.com/retirement/how-plan-medical-expenses-retirement/
- *10 Best Low-Risk Investments Right Now* https://www.forbes.com/advisor/investing/best-low-risk-investments/
- *Ultimate Guide to Senior Discounts and Where to Find Them* https://www.moneygeek.com/financial-planning/resources/guide-to-senior-discounts-and-deals/
- *The Mental Health Benefits of Socializing for Seniors* https://www.seniorlifestyle.com/resources/blog/the-mental-health-benefits-of-socializing-for-seniors/
- *How To Use Skype: A Simple Guide For Seniors | TerraBella* https://www.terrabellaseniorliving.com/senior-living-blog/how-to-use-skype-a-simple-guide-for-seniors/
- *11 Meaningful Ways Older Adults Can Volunteer Right Now* https://www.forbes.com/health/healthy-aging/volunteer-opportunities-for-older-adults/
- *8 Online Communities for Seniors to Join* https://www.makeuseof.com/online-communities-for-seniors/
- *The Best Smart Home Devices to Help Aging in Place* https://www.nytimes.com/wirecutter/reviews/smart-home-for-seniors/
- *The Senior's Guide to Online Safety* https://connectsafely.org/seniors-guide-to-online-safety/
- *Best Social Media Apps for Seniors and How to Use Them ...* https://www.seniorhelpers.com/fl/south-palm-beach/resources/blogs/best-social-media-apps-for-seniors-and-how-to-use-them-safely/
- *5 Sites With Online Classes for Seniors to Keep Learning* https://www.centerforasecureretirement.com/posts/5-sites-with-online-classes-for-seniors-to-keep-learning
- *Hobbies protect older people from age-related decline in ...* https://www.news-medical.net/news/20230911/Hobbies-protect-older-

people-from-age-related-decline-in-mental-health-and-wellbeing.aspx

- *Smartphone Photography – Senior Planet from AARP* https://seniorplanet.org/course/smartphone-photography/
- *Gardening For Retirees: A Senior Hobby For Growth And ...* https://memorycherish.com/gardening-for-retirees/
- *Art Programs for Adults* https://www.mocanomi.org/learn/adults
- *Thrifty Strategies for Senior Travelers* https://www.nytimes.com/2022/09/22/travel/frugal-strategies-for-senior-travelers.html
- *Travel Discounts for Seniors | Retirement* https://money.usnews.com/money/retirement/aging/articles/travel-discounts-for-seniors
- *Retirement Destinations For Culture And Arts* https://retirementlivingmag.com/retirement-destinations-for-culture-and-arts/
- *How To Get Pre-Existing Conditions Covered By Travel ...* https://www.forbes.com/advisor/travel-insurance/pre-existing-conditions/
- *Downsizing For Seniors: Complete Guide With Checklist* https://www.storypoint.com/resources/senior-living/downsizing-for-seniors/
- *Home Safety for Older Adults: A Comprehensive Guide 2024* https://www.ncoa.org/adviser/sleep/home-safety-older-adults/
- *5 Health Benefits of Living in a Green Retirement Community* https://sustainablelivingassociation.org/5-health-benefits-of-living-in-a-green-retirement-community/
- *How to choose energy-efficient appliances – a 9-step guide* https://www.homesandgardens.com/kitchens/how-to-choose-energy-efficient-appliances
- *Intergenerational programs: What can school-age children ...* https://www.ncbi.nlm.nih.gov/pmc/articles/PMC6728408/
- *Surefire Ways to Connect Kids and Grandparents via ...* https://neafamily.com/your-family/parenting/surefire-ways-to-connect-kids-and-grandparents-via-technolog/
- *8 Legacy Project Ideas For Seniors To Leave A Lasting ...* https://www.storii.com/blog/legacy-project-ideas-for-seniors
- *Bridging the Generation Gap: Ideas for Intergenerational ...* https://www.grandvillaclearwater.com/senior-living/fl/clearwater/blog/bridging-the-generation-gap-ideas-for-intergenerational-activities
- *How Creativity Benefits Mind, Body and Soul in Seniors* https://

seniorlivinginstyle.com/blog/health-wellness/how-creativity-benefits-mind-body-and-soul-in-seniors/

- *How to Write a Memoir: Examples and a Step-by-Step Guide* https://writers.com/how-to-write-a-memoir
- *Online Learning and Digital Content Creation for Older Adults* https://theaging.ai/articles/digital-content-creation-for-older-adults/#:~:text=For%20video%20production%20and%20edit-ing,and%20engaging%20with%20the%20audience.
- *Older Adult Community Programs - Mather* https://www.mather.com/programs
- *Organizing your Community for Aging in Place* https://naipc.memberclicks.net/assets/docs/Organizing%20Your%20Community-Toolkit.pdf
- *Advocacy with older people: Some practical suggestions* https://www.helpage.org/silo/files/advocacy-with-older-people-some-practical-suggestions-.pdf
- *The Ultimate Nonprofit Event Planning Checklist for Success* https://bloomerang.co/blog/nonprofit-event-planning-checklist/
- *Inspirational initiatives that keep elderly people active* https://www.thegoodcaregroup.com/news/inspirational-initiatives-keep-elderly-people-active/
- *How to Sign Up: A Guide to Medicare Enrollment* https://www.aarp.org/health/medicare-insurance/info-2020/enrolling-in-medicare.html
- *The Big Choice: Original Medicare vs. Medicare Advantage* https://www.aarp.org/health/medicare-insurance/info-2020/original-medicare-vs-advantage.html
- *Your Guide to Medicare Preventive Services* https://www.medicare.gov/publications/10110-Your-Guide-to-Medicare-Preventive-Services.pdf
- *Find Healthcare Providers: Compare Care Near You | ...* https://www.medicare.gov/care-compare/
- *The Benefits Of Writing A Gratitude Journal As You Age* https://www.rittenhousevillages.com/assisted-living-blog/the-benefits-of-writing-a-gratitude-journal-as-you-age/
- *How to Start a Scholarship Fund in 5 Simple Steps* https://bold.org/blog/irs-guidelines-for-starting-a-scholarship-fund/
- *Mindfulness-Based Interventions for Older Adults* https://www.ncbi.nlm.nih.gov/pmc/articles/PMC4868399/

- *Who Is Your Successful Aging Role Model? - Oxford Academic*
  https://academic.oup.com/psychsocgerontology/article/72/2/237/
  2374923